D0180142

MEDITATION
FOR
WARRIORS

OTHER BOOKS BY LOREN W. CHRISTENSEN

These books are available on Amazon, from their publishers, and through the usual book outlets. Some are available as ebooks. Signed copies can be purchased at LWC Books, www.lwcbooks.com

Nonfiction

Street Stoppers	Fighting In The Clinch
Fighter's Fact Book	Fighter's Fact Book 2
Solo Training	Solo Training 2
Speed Training	The Fighter's Body
Total Defense	The Mental Edge
The Way Alone	Far Beyond Defensive Tactics
Fighting Power	Crouching Tiger
Anything Goes	Winning With American Kata
Total Defense	Riot
Warriors	On Combat
Warrior Mindset	Deadly Force Encounters
Surviving Workplace Violence	Surviving A School Shooting
Gangbangers	Skinhead Street Gangs
Hookers, Tricks And Cops	Way Of The Warrior
Skid Row Beat	Defensive Tactics
Missing Children	Self-Defense For Women
Extreme Joint Locking	Timing In The Martial Arts

Fighter's Guide to Hard-Core Heavy Bag Training
The Brutal Art Of Ripping, Poking And Pressing Vital Targets
How To Live Safely In A Dangerous World
Fighting The Pain Resistant Attacker
Evolution of Weaponry

Fiction

Dukkha: The Suffering	Dukkha: Reverb

MEDITATION
FOR
WARRIORS

Practical Meditation for Cops,
Soldiers and Martial Artists

LOREN W. CHRISTENSEN

Copyright © 2013 Loren W. Christensen

All rights reserved

Do not reproduce in any form without permission.

For permissions, more information, or to reach the author, contact:

LWC BOOKS
PO Box 20311
Portland, Oregon
97294-0311
lwcbooks.com
sales@lwcbooks.com

Cover and Interior Design by Kamila Z. Miller
Background for the cover by Sirius-sdz
  http://sirius-sdz.deviantart.com/

ISBN 10: 1490594035
ISBN 13: 978-1490594033

Neither the author nor the publisher assumes any responsibility for the use or misuse of this book.

ACKNOWLEDGEMENTS

As always, much love to Lisa Place for her support and patience over the years.

Thanks to the many people who told me about their meditation practice. I've noted them all by name after their quotes.

Thanks to Afghanistan war veteran and martial artist Kevin Faulk for his eagle eye at spotting errors in the manuscript.

CONTENTS

Note: For ease of writing and reading, the word(s):

"Soldiers" denotes the brave men and women in all military branches.

"Cops" and "police" denote the brave men and women in all law enforcement agencies.

"Martial artists" denotes the hard training men and women in the all styles and systems.

SECTION I

"Meditate, Visualize and Create your own reality ..." – Amit Ray

INTRODUCTION

WHAT THIS BOOK IS AND ISN'T

Of all the things I've lost, I miss my mind the most.
~ Mark Twain

No woo-woo found here

To meditate, you don't need to follow a particular religion, espouse New Age theories and beliefs, bow to a guru, sensei, sifu, or a robed and bearded guide. Nor do you need to burn incense, rub crystals, or imagine yourself flying through a starlit sky on the wing of a butterfly. You can do these things if you want but you don't have to. I mean no disrespect toward people who practice and benefit from such disciplines. I know many who do and they are fine people. I only mention it from the get-go because many believe that is what meditation is about. It isn't.

The only equipment you need is—nothing. Everything you need to meditate you have right now, including this small guide. A quiet place is beneficial, especially at first, but you will learn techniques to meditate in noisy ones too.

So in short, you can meditate everyday and still hang out with your military pals, cop buddies, and fellow martial arts students. You can still own a pit bull, drive a Harley, and share lies with your drinking buddies. The same is true whether you're a firefighter, doorman, bodyguard, medic, security officer, or lion tamer.

The fact is, meditation will make you better at all these things.

Simplicity found here

I like things to be simple, especially definitions. For example, I've always liked the late 10th-degree black belt, Peter Urban's definition of karate: "The art of fightin' real good." I couldn't agree more.

I've written many books on the fighting arts and not one of them is complicated. Simplicity is the common thread for one very important reason. In my 29 years in law enforcement, which includes my years in the Army as a Military Policeman with a year in Vietnam, and as a martial artist since 1965, it has been my experience that it's simplicity that wins the battle. Fighting is just too fast and furious for techniques and concepts that are fancy schmancy or, I'll say it one last time, woo-woo.

Meditation is simple. So for our definition, let's strip it to its essence. Let's say that meditation is the act of— drum roll, please—doing nothing. Okay, you have to do something: you got to sit quietly, or stand quietly, or walk quietly. But that's it.

That said, too many gurus, sifus, and other teachers teach complex meditation methods because they either think people want that or they believe that complexity is somehow better. Not so.

Meditation is simple, regardless of how people try to complicate it.

My history

No one has ever accused me of being a touch-feely, tie-dyed T-shirt wearing, granola eating kind of guy. Because I'm not. I've been training hard in the martial arts for nearly five decades, I'm a war veteran, and I'm a retired street cop. As an author, I've written multiple books on the warrior lifestyle, non-fiction and fiction. No, I'm not even a little touchy-feely. Nonetheless, I have enjoyed the benefits of meditation for more than two decades.

While researching a book in 1989, I was introduced to the power of self-hypnosis by three people: an acupuncturist, a therapist/martial artist, and a psychologist for the Oregon Trail Blazers basketball team. In the early 1990s, I learned how to practice mental imagery from a number of writers, from a police psychologist friend, and from the teachings of Chuck Norris. Some years later, my lady and I learned meditation at a Zen temple and a Zen monastery. Most recently, I've learned from a Taiwanese monk.

I'm not a sage sitting in front of a high mountain cave. I'm just a guy who has lived (survived) a warrior lifestyle who now passes on what he's learned.

A Simple Meditation To Get You Started

I encourage you to read this book from the front to the back, rather than jumping around impatiently (meditation will help with your impatience). But if you're in a hurry (meditation will help you slow down too), to experience meditation, here is an easy one you can do as you work your way through the book. Oh, by the way, this has been taught to the Marines. Oorah!

A 5-minute meditation to get a little relaxed

Sit comfortably on a cushion in your home, in a quiet corner in your training facility, on a tree stump in the forest, or on a vehicle fender. You will use your hands to find tension above your eyebrows, around your jaw, in your neck, and in your shoulders. You will spend 30 seconds on each location rubbing the tension away as you mentally relax the tightness with your thoughts.

Here is how to do this simple procedure:

- To begin feeling relaxed, sit comfortably with your hands in your lap or on your thighs, and breathe in slowly and deeply. Then exhale slowly. Focus your mind on your breaths. Feel your breath enter through your nose and feel it exit out your mouth. Do four of these exchanges.
- Now, as you breathe normally, touch the fingers of both hands to each eyebrow. Massage them in slow circles for 30 seconds as you mentally relax your forehead and eyes. Put your hands back in your lap.

- Inhale slowly, as you mentally feel how relaxed your forehead has become, and exhale slowly as you mentally relax it even more.
- Breathe normally as you touch the sides of your jaw with the fingers of both hands, and lightly and slowly massage it in small circles for 30 seconds as you mentally relax it. Put your hands back in your lap.
- Inhale slowly as you mentally feel how relaxed your jaw is, and exhale slowly as you mentally relax it even more.
- Breathe normally as you touch the back of your neck with the fingers of both hands, and lightly and slowly massage it in small circles for 30 seconds as you mentally relax it. Put your hands back in your lap.
- Inhale slowly as you mentally feel how relaxed your neck is, and exhale slowly as you mentally relax it even more.
- Breathe normally as you touch the muscles on the tops of your shoulders near the base of your neck with the fingers of both hands. Lightly massage in small circles for 30 seconds as you mentally relax the two points. Put your hands back in your lap.
- Inhale slowly as you mentally feel how relaxed both of your shoulders are, and then exhale slowly as you mentally relax them even more.

Take one minute to mentally scan these points. Inhale as you feel each point in your mind and exhale feeling them relax even more. It will take about 10 seconds to do this with each location.

That's it. Feeling mellow now?

CHAPTER 1

13 COMMON MYTHS ABOUT MEDITATION

"Beware of false knowledge, it is more dangerous than ignorance" ~ Bernard Shaw

Stripped to its bare essence, meditation is a moment of mental quiet.

That's pretty much it.

Unfortunately, there are lots of myths surrounding it. Sadly, some people buy into one or more of these without hesitation and without questioning. Here are a few common ones.

Myth 1: Meditation is hard

No way. Hard means that something takes a lot of effort, lots of stress, and days, weeks and months of strenuous work. But when done as suggested in this book, meditation is not only easy, it's one of the most enjoyable things you will ever do.

It's effortless because, well, you're not doing anything. And when you're not doing anything, there isn't anything to force. When you don't have anything to force, there is no stress. In short, meditation is all about relaxing, calmness, and peace.

Myth 2: Meditation is a religion

No. Meditation might look like prayer—sitting, standing, or walking quietly—and people from many different religions do enjoy the benefits of it, but it doesn't follow a higher being or advocate any particular faith, or even the absence of faith.

If it were a religion, this would be the bible:

> Chapter 1: Sit
> Chapter 2: Breathe
> The end.

Myth 3: You must stop your thinking

Not so, because you can't. Thinking is what your mind does just as seeing is what your eyes do. Can you stop your open eyes from seeing? No. Nor can you stop your mind from thinking.

When meditating, you simply acknowledge a thought that enters your mind, and let it go. Then you do it again with the next thought that enters and again with the next. In time, your thoughts will slow. But they won't stop.

Myth 4: You go into a trance

Not true. Meditation is simply a way to calm the mind and ultimately achieve clarity of thought. If you see someone walking about with stars in their eyes and their arms extended in front of them, they got something else going on: they're sleep walking, they're high on dope, or they might be a zombie. But they aren't meditating.

Myth 5: You're unable to meditate because you can't calm your mind

Sometimes your mind becomes peaceful quickly when meditating, while other times it's a mess and jumps all about like a monkey on LSD. Meditators, in fact, call this "monkey mind."

Whether your mind is calm or you're having a monkey mind moment, it's okay. Where a problem arises is when you try to fight whatever is going on in your head. But when you learn to go with the flow and not fight the monkey— be it boredom, anger, agitation, general turbulence—your mind is much more likely to settle down.

Myth 6: Meditation is an altered state of consciousness

Your mind will be altered, in that it will be less cluttered and confused. Meditation leads to a more focused and patient mind.

Myth 7: Meditation stops when you open your eyes

The act of meditation might stop but the benefits continue. After just a few sessions, you begin feeling the benefits 24/7, such as when you're at home with your family, shopping at the mall, working out in your gym, training at the dojo, or plinking with your .50 cal out at the firing range.

Myth 8: It takes a long time to benefit

You start benefiting from meditation the first time you do it. You might not feel peace and clarity of thought right off, but after one or two meditation sessions, your body and mind will begin to enjoy relief from stress.

Myth 9: You have to sit in lotus position

I can't sit in lotus (cross legged with each foot on the opposite thigh) and many people I've sat with over the years can't either, or simply don't want to. In the west, we meditate in chairs, on cushions, with our back against a tree, while perched on a vehicle fender, an airplane wing, in a squad car, and while walking and lying down. That said, if you're flexible in the hips and you can sit in lotus without a problem, go ahead.

The most important thing is that you find a position that is comfortable for you.

Myth 10: Meditation is for old people

Yes, as well as middle-aged folks and young people. Kids are doing it now and report wonderful results. One middle school student said she doesn't get so angry anymore since she has been meditating. A teenager said that he enjoys the calmness he feels throughout his day after a session.

Myth 11: You only meditate at certain times and in certain places

No. I have meditated before the sun has come up in the morning and I've meditated at midnight. I've done it in a Zen monastery, in the back of a van packed with heavily armed cops on the way to raid a gangbanger's house, and I've meditated in line at the grocery. Most recently, I did it at the dentist where, let's call him Dr. Pain, was showing me no mercy.

Some people prefer sunrise. I know one meditator, a boxer and martial artist, who arises daily around 4 in the morning and meditates until 7 (no, you don't have to meditate that long). I usually meditate just before going to bed. It doesn't matter when you do it as long as it works for you.

Myth 12: The most common form of meditation is Transcendental Meditation

I've never done it. It's a well-known method because of the Beatles and other celebrities. Experts say that this is a relatively minor form of meditation and can be quite expensive. The methods you learn here are the most common and don't cost a dime.

Myth 13: Meditation has to be practiced under supervision

A teacher can be quite helpful, but anyone can learn the techniques in this book without prior training. With willingness to try and a little discipline to stick with it, you will be meditating and enjoying the benefits after only a few sessions.

CHAPTER 2

WHY WARRIORS NEED MEDITATION

*Meditation is a lot like doing reps at a gym.
It strengthens your attention muscle ~ David Levy*

There are a couple of mindsets among some warriors that are happily diminishing as we move deeper into the 21st century. The first is the "suck it up" mindset. A cop or military warrior is involved in a life and death battle and afterwards the powers that be, and sometimes the individual's peers, tell him or her to "suck it up" and get back in the saddle. The other belief is that harnessing the power of the mind is New Age and a bunch of b.s. made up by hippies and granola eaters.

This kind of thinking is going away with retirements. In addition, there is a growing knowledge of the critical importance of ensuring that participants who have experienced in-your-face violence get the help they need—professional counseling, peer counseling, peer and professional debriefing, or simply time to collect themselves—so they can return to being productive members of their organization.

For as long as there has been written and recorded human history, there has been meditation, and not just by Buddhist monks sitting in temples or sages sitting on a high mountaintop. Meditation is a nonsectarian activity, meaning that Buddhists do it, as well as Zen practitioners, Christians, Jews, Moslems, and atheists. Rich people do it, poor people, alternative lifestyle people, and corporate CEOs. Top athletes meditate, such as summer and winter Olympic competitors from every event. Martial artists have used meditation for as long as there have been kung fu kicks and judo flips. In recent years, the military and law enforcement have discovered the extraordinary value of meditating, though there is still some stigma attached. The good news is that the stigma is going away.

Recently, I attended an archery tournament and saw a competitor meditating before his match. Not surprisingly, his first shot hit dead center and his follow-up arrows nearly hit the first one.

Warriors Use It Because It Works

One Army veteran discovered the power of meditation from another soldier. He told me:

> "*There was a soldier in Afghanistan into the Zen/hippie stuff. He was always meditating, doing yoga, whatever. Thing is, he always seemed so calm no matter what was going on. So I asked him to show me how to meditate. After awhile, it started to make a huge difference on how I mentally dealt with stress in combat.*"

A weapon or strategy that doesn't work on a battlefield of war is quickly discarded. Police tools come and go, but those that remain do so because they work. While veteran martial artists have learned a large number of techniques and fighting concepts, the ones they take into that proverbial dark alley are the simple, basic ones that have withstood the test of time. Likewise, meditation has lasted since early-recorded history for one reason—it's simple and it works.

Here is what my friend Paul McRedmond, a veteran martial artist, retired police officer, and a guy who has practiced meditation since the 1970s, wrote in an email exchange.

> "*The nervous system can only take so much dynamic input before it crashes/needs to sleep, etc. It's like filling a cup with water. The cup can actually take more water than just the cup's measure. But one more drop can cause more water to flow from the cup than just that one drop. Loren, you've dealt with many, many 'last straw' (last drop of stress) people. With them, a seemingly random event, a*

single word or a glance can cause emotional upset, panic, screaming, and, sometimes, really stupid actions.

"Even cops are susceptible to this last drop syndrome. A great cop, decorated, always calm, and a problem solver, suddenly beats a suspect beyond what was needed to gain control. And, of course, he gets into trouble. If you were to look into his professional and personal life, you will find a full cup of water.

"An empty cup means the ability to accept and thus deal with input. The emptier the cup, the more input/ stress you can receive and process.

"There are three ways to empty your cup: You can get a bigger one. You can dump or drain the water in the existing one, or you can avoid water. Training, relationships, good nutrition, and exercise all enlarge the cup. Sleep allows some of the water to drain and vacations get you away from the water.

"But, meditation does all three at once. It expands the capacity of your nervous system by creating coherence (a synergistic pattern of brain wave frequencies across the 4 main quadrants of the brain), it allows for greater restfulness during sleep (draining the water), and (here comes the woo-woo stuff) to eventually become water."

Bryan Ward, a cop in New Zealand, a long-time martial artist, and meditator, said this about his practice:

"My meditation objective is to be calmer and to assist with my practice in aikido and krav maga. I generally sit between 10 and 20 minutes every day in the morning. What I have found is that if a meditation method works for you, then use it. I have seen some other styles of practice that I have initially thought nonsense, such as focusing on dolphin sounds, Indian shaman chanting,

*and so on. But if at the end of the day it works for you...
then it works."*

Let's begin by looking at just a few of the benefits of
meditation for today's combat warrior. Understand that
as your meditation practice continues, you will discover
additional benefits specific to your needs.

Benefits Of A Calm Mind

Do you see yourself in any of these issues?

Do you get easily nervous before:
   going on a police call?
   working a military mission?
   testing for a martial arts belt?
   competing?

Do you get easily irritated:
   at your boss, superiors, trainers, peers?

Do you have fears and doubts about:
   your performance in training?
   your performance in a real situation?

Do you have difficulties falling asleep at night because of:
   your concerns about your skill set, or lack there of?
   your training progress?
   how you compare to others?
   your physical issues?

Do certain thoughts keep obsessing your mind, such as:
   your ability to perform in certain situations?
   past errors?
   the effects of past traumatic incidents?
   the opinion of others?

Do you have difficulty focusing your mind on:
your training?
   your objectives?
   the situation?
   instructions?

There are numerous benefits to calming the mind. Here are just a few that can help your study, training, and performance.

Better sleep
Clearer focus
Greater effectiveness
Anger control
Anxiety control
Ability to learn faster
Stress release
Less distraction
Better concentration
Reduced depression
Enhanced physical relaxation

All you need to know about brainwaves

Normally, you go about your daily routine in beta brainwaves, which can be physically and mentally draining. When you attain alpha and theta brainwaves on a regular basis through calming meditation, not only do you get an energy boost (most children are regularly in alpha and theta, which explains their seemingly endless energy), you also get improved memory, increased concentration, greater relaxation, and a general overall feeling of happiness.

The *aah* factor

A Zen teacher once asked me why I sit, that is, why do I sit on a cushion and meditate. Without hesitation, I answered, "For the *aah*." There were about 20 people present, all veteran meditators, and every one of them smiled and nodded because they knew exactly what *"aah"* meant.

You know what it is too. That first day on vacation when you settle into a comfortable beach chair, look out at the ocean, and take that first sip of mai tai. That's an *aah*. Or that moment after a killer training session and you're back home, showered, dressed in your favorite sweat pants and T-shirt, and you collapse onto your sofa, remote in hand. *Aah*, life is good.

Once you're in the groove of meditation, that *aah* moment is one of the pluses that greet you. Okay, not every time, but nearly. Sometimes it's tough to meditate, but as will be discussed, even a tough session is still beneficial.

When you get into your meditation position—sitting in a Zen monastery, sitting on the floor at the beginning of a martial arts class, riding in a military vehicle on a dusty road in Afghanistan, or sitting in a police car behind an empty warehouse—that *ahh* begins the physical and mental processes to make you a better warrior.

Calming to improve learning ability

It's difficult to learn new information and skills when your mind is anxious, frightened, confused, angry, and bouncing all over the place as it deals with an assortment of other issues. Conversely, a mind that is calm, collected, and receptive learns more easily, more quickly, and more deeply. A calm mind absorbs and remembers. An agitated mind, doesn't. It's as simple as that.

To prepare for a high-risk task

Whether you're preparing for a grueling martial arts competition, a drug raid with a SWAT team, or a house-to-house search for enemy insurgents, meditation will ready you for the task by calming your mind and body. This in turn gives you clarity of thought and greater control over your physical actions, so that all of your hard training will be readily available to you.

Perform better

When asked how meditation helped his martial arts and his job as a bodyguard, one man told me:

> *"It has enhanced everything in my life, to include but not limited to, focusing, better retention of my training and studies, and better decision-making processing."*

Doesn't get much better than that.

Greater physical and mental control under stress

Mike Tyson once said, "Everyone has a plan until they get punched in the face." When I was in Vietnam, the expression was, "A battle plan is excellent until the first shot is fired." While there is a lot of truth to these, it doesn't have to be that way. Meditation, and your resultant calm and controlled mind, will help you maintain that plan and to better apply your training.

A veteran sheriff's deputy and 40-year martial arts veteran told me that one of the primary benefits he has achieved from meditation is, in his words:

"Emotional equilibrium, especially in the midst of screaming-profane-arm-waving-finger-pointing-blood-and-guts."

In other words, he is able to stay calm and collected when the you-know-what hits the hydro-electric powered oscillating air current distribution device, i.e., the fan.

Unwind after the event and recover better

I've coauthored two books—*Deadly Force Encounters* and *On Combat*—in which police officers and soldiers told my coauthors and me that the worst part of their traumatic encounters was the aftermath, the hours, days, weeks, and months that followed their incidents. Those who have problems often complain of uncontrolled thoughts, reliving the incident 24/7, poor sleep, uncontrolled anger, depression, and many other issues.

Meditation will dramatically reduce these symptoms, which is why it's so often prescribed to sufferers.

Meditating on

Meditating on something is a powerful tool that reaps incredible results. When you meditate on an issue—your shooting skills, front kick, handcuffing techniques—you're able to look more intensely and more deeply at it than you ever have before. By first preparing your mind by becoming quiet, still, and intensely relaxed, you're able to see an issue deeply without interference from random thoughts and other distractions.

I have practiced meditating on a particular thing many times. Most recently, I meditated on my fiction writing. I had dug my lead character into a hole and I couldn't figure out how to get him out. Another time, I was stuck as to how a particular scene should unfold. By meditating on these things, I found the solution.

Sometimes I meditate on an issue while sitting in front of my computer and other times I go into a room in our home that is used for meditating. I get comfortable, close my eyes, and focus on my breath as I strive to get my mind and body as relaxed as possible. Once I've achieved this state and my thoughts have slowed and I feel a sense of quiet and calm in both mind and body, I begin to meditate on my issue.

So far, every time I've done it I have found the solution to my problem. Of course, there might be an occasion down the road where I won't find an answer. When that happens, I'll just try it again the next day. I already know that it works but some issues just might take more than one session.

Can Meditation Replace Sleep?

The boxer friend I mentioned earlier, the man with decades of daily meditation experience, says that he sleeps less because he meditates. He routinely gets up long before the sun and meditates until long after it's risen. He says that among other benefits, it energizes him for his day, the same as does seven or eight hours of sleep for other people. While we can't argue with how he feels, it can be said that maybe he feels rested and energized because his four or five hours of sleep is all his body and brain require. While most people need to sleep more, some people function just fine on less than the often-recommended eight hours.

But this isn't true for everyone.

Your body needs sufficient sleep to rejuvenate and repair, which is especially important when you're training hard on running, weight training, martial arts, police tactics, and military training. When you're sleeping, your body releases hormones that help your muscles repair and grow, form white blood cells, fight all those diseases constantly attacking your body, maintain your svelte physique, make new skin cells, and help you to avoid premature aging.

Meditation slows your brain into a relaxed state: that alpha brain wave discussed earlier. It creates peacefulness, profound relaxation, and mental clarity, and it does so faster than a nap. Because meditation induces a state of mental bliss, if you will, and a deep sense of calmness, it gives you the physical benefits associated with reduced stress.

But wait! Because these things are all done while you're in a state called "mental wakefulness," it doesn't do the same things that sleep does, such as the physical repair and various rejuvenation type tasks that occur *only* when you're asleep.

Lose too much sleep, and you're at risk for loss of memory, mental confusion, high blood pressure, additional pounds around the midsection, muscle fatigue, vulnerability to injury, and susceptibility to illness.

While meditation is not a replacement for quality shuteye, sleep and meditation do compliment each other. Get sufficient sleep and you enjoy better meditation sessions. Include regular meditation in your life and you sleep more deeply and enjoy greater rejuvenation.

More on all these issues as you move through the book.

CHAPTER 3

NUTS AND BOLTS

"Your mind is an instrument, a tool, [a weapon]"
~Eckhart Tolle

Before we get into the various methods let's look at what I call the nuts and bolts of meditation. Consider this the foundation from which you will make adjustments, add to, delete from, or simply use as is. What you do and how you do it might not work for your husband or wife, your buddy, your students, your teachers, or the milkman. Or it might very well work for all of them. What does matter is that it works for you.

There are many ways to meditate. Some are quite simplistic. Some are far more complex for what most of us need. You won't find the latter here. Think of the various meditation methods that follow as tools or devices to help you accomplish something, i.e., relax, increase your awareness, control your anxiety, feel a sense of peace, and so on. By the time you get through all of the ones described herein, you'll have the tools needed to help you find the right method to get what you want out of meditation.

Set, Sit, And Forget

Dr. Timothy Storlie is a friend, a doctor of psychology, a martial artist, and a meditator since prehistoric animals roamed the Earth. Here is what he calls "Set, Sit, and Forget," which I've edited just a tad to fit our needs.

"You may already have a relaxation and meditation practice that works. If so, great! Keep it up. Do What Works! But if you don't have a practice yet (or just want to try something new) here's an easy one that I do every day. I call it Set, Sit, and Forget.

Set: "Mentally set your intention. For example, "Sitting here makes me feel more calm, centered and relaxed."

Sit: "Sit down and close your eyes. Put the tip of your tongue on the roof of your mouth and leave it there for the duration. Gently place your attention on your belly or heart area (just be aware of it, the sensation of it). Focus on it lightly. No stress or strain.

Forget: "Forget about whatever you think you have to do, need to do, or should do. Don't try to relax. Don't try to meditate. Don't try to stop your thoughts. Forget about all of that and just breathe. Whenever you become aware that your attention or awareness has drifted away from your belly or heart area, just gently guide it back. Do this for 5 to 15 minutes until you feel calm, centered, and relaxed. At the peak of this relaxation, connect your feeling with the trigger words, 'I feel calm, centered, and relaxed.'

"In the future, when you sit down to meditate, slowly repeat these words to yourself a few times to deepen your experience. Hint: You can also use these trigger words to help re-enter this relaxed state any other time you might need to.

"I read somewhere that there's a phrase used in some Tibetan traditions that describes the optimum state of awareness and relaxation as "sitting like an old man basking in the sun." This really does sum it all up. No intent or desire to go anywhere or do anything else other than to just sit and enjoy wherever you are at that precise moment."

Dr. Storlie mentioned, "trigger words." We'll talk more about them shortly. But here is a teaser: They are incredibly powerful.

Keep It Positive

Did you notice how positive Dr. Storlie's comments are when he first sits? *"Sitting here makes me feel more calm, centered and relaxed."* An example of stating this negatively would be "Sitting here doesn't make me feel stressed, crazy, and tense." It might seem like it's the same thing—but it isn't. Many experts think that your subconscious can't hear the word "doesn't." Therefore, it hears only, "Sitting here makes me feel stressed, crazy, and tense." Clearly, this isn't a good thing. So keep your statements positive. More on this later.

Where To Do It

Short answer: anywhere you want. It doesn't matter as long as it works for you. Quick, relatively shallow sessions, say, 2 minutes to 10 minutes, can be done in the most adverse of places and circumstances: in an alleyway, on a stakeout, in a crowd, and so on. Longer sessions, say 20 to 30 minutes, are usually done in a quiet and comfortable setting: a room void of people and distractions, a clearing in a forest, a quiet car.

Here are some of the places I've done it.

Sitting

Cushion: Typically, we think of a meditator sitting on a cushion, legs folded in a joint-destroying entanglement, one hand resting in the palm of the other, thumbs touching, back ramrod straight, and face calm and at peace. This method is common in temples and monasteries. I do it this way at home because that is how I've trained and I don't have a problem with it.

Chair: Some people in temples and monasteries opt to sit in chairs, most often because of age limitations or some kind of injury. When I used to sit in a Zen temple, I called these folks "chair people." I wasn't being derogatory; I was just trying to be funny. Then I hurt my leg training and I couldn't sit on a cushion for a while. So I became…one of them. But the joke was on me because I discovered quickly that it wasn't much easier than sitting on a cushion. While my legs weren't tied in a knot, I had to sit on the front edge of the chair (a requirement of the temple), with an unsupported straight back, and hands folded together.

Car: You can meditate in your parked car while waiting for someone, while staking out a location or person, during your lunch break, while waiting to execute a warrant, or while parked in a turnout overlooking a beautiful view. I've done it in all of these places.

Meditating while riding as a passenger is easy to do. You can do it in the passenger seat in front, in the back, or way in the back if you're riding on a bus, plane, or train. If you're a white-knuckle flier, meditation and the resultant calming is a wonderful antidote and cheaper than airline booze.

I once meditated in the back of a van while sitting on a tire with several other cops all around me. We were part of a caravan of vehicles, on the way to raid a house in which we knew the occupants were armed. It was oh-dark-thirty and many of the officers were hyped on bad coffee and anticipation. The closer we got to the target, the quieter it got in the van. Without closing my eyes, I began a silent 4-count breathing technique (discussed later) to cool my adrenaline and to slow my heart rate. No one had a clue I was doing it and when we screeched to a stop and the doors burst open, I was calm, collected, and good to go.

Standing

Anytime you're in line—movie theater, chow hall, roll call, grocery—and you're alone, seize the opportunity to meditate lightly to bring on a moment of calm. No, it doesn't always have to be a quiet place. Read on.

The first time I did it standing, I was outside the doors of an abortion clinic trying to prevent an angry mob from gaining entry. I was the first officer to arrive at a massive brawl between pro-choice and anti-abortion people. Because fists were flying and protest signs were clobbering,

I pushed through the mob without waiting for backup. After knocking a couple of people down who had swung signs at me, I found myself with my back against the locked doors of the clinic as the mob pushed against me in their effort to force their way inside.

My hands were shaking, my thumping heart was making my badge bounce, and my eyes were watering so badly that I could barely see. During a short lull in the pushing and shoving, I began 4-count breathing (discussed later) without anyone knowing. By the second cycle, my hands stopped shaking, my heart rate moved below the danger zone, and my vision improved. After the third cycle, I was once again in control of myself, and able to calm those closest to me as I stalled, waiting for my backup.

I've also done standing meditation while on a guard post, waiting to speak to an audience, waiting to be reamed by a supervisor, and while pacing in anticipation of being called out to compete in a martial arts tournament.

Walking

We will describe in detail in Chapter 6 how to do walking meditation. For now, just know that it's easy, it's immensely rewarding, and it's a nice break from meditating in a sitting position. You can do it barefoot, in running shoes, or in combat boots. The only requirement is that you do it in a place where you aren't going to walk into traffic, walk over the side of a battleship, or walk in front of a jet.

Lying down

The "risk" when meditating lying down is that you might fall asleep. If you nod off easily but you want to meditate for a while, you're going to have to do it sitting, standing, or walking.

However, if you have trouble sleeping at night, you might find that some of the relaxation inducing techniques help you drift off. While this isn't meditation, per se, many people find that the relaxation phase helps them get that much needed shuteye. More on this Chapter 9: Meditate to Induce Sleep.

How Long Should You Meditate?

There are many schools of thought on this. I spent a long weekend at a Zen monastery once where we meditated for 25 minutes at a time. When the gong sounded that the time was up, we stood on stiff and cramped legs, and walked in a large circle for 5 minutes while—you guessed it—meditating. We then resumed sitting for another 25 minutes. This was repeated all daylong, a day that began at 5:00 in the morning and ended at 8:00 at night. There were a couple of times when I thought my kneecaps were going to blow out of my legs and roll across the floor like loose hubcaps.

No, you don't have to meditate to that extent or even close to it.

In the beginning, meditate for five minutes and then, after two or three weeks, go for ten. There is no rush to add time. In fact, there is no *rushing* anywhere in meditation. Don't put pressure on yourself; meditation is about alleviating pressure and stress. If after a month or so you want to increase your meditation time or the number of times you do it throughout your day, that's fine. Or do it when you feel like it. Today you might feel like meditating three times for 15 or 20 minutes but tomorrow you feel like doing it for one five-minute session. No problem. As the saying goes: It's all good.

When Is The Best Time?

Some meditation gurus believe there are specific times during the 24-hour day when it's best to meditate. We'll leave that to the monastery monks. For the rest of us, the answer is this: anytime is a good time. If you like doing it the morning, great. Just before bedtime, great. On your coffee breaks, great.

But try not to do it when you're really hungry or right after eating. Noisy hunger pangs can be disruptive as can noisy digestion. Additionally, sitting right after eating can compress your esophagus, which can cause acid reflux or heartburn.

How To Breathe—Correctly

Here is the thing about punching: Do it wrong and you can hit pretty hard. But do it correctly, you can hit a lot harder and with less chance of breaking your hand. It's the same with breathing. You can breathe improperly and make it through your life in one piece. But when you do it right, you will make it through your life much healthier and calmer.

Breathing incorrectly

Breathing incorrectly can negatively affect your body, including your immune, circulatory, endocrine and nervous systems. Improper breathing can produce a variety of symptoms, including:

Fuzzy thinking
Lightheadedness
Emotionlessness
Apprehension
Chest pain
Digestive problems
Irritable bowel
Neck and shoulder pain

Clearly, these symptoms aren't anything anyone wants, especially a warrior.

Breathing correctly

On the flip side, proper breathing affects—in a good way—virtually every part of your body. When you properly oxygenate your system, you revitalize your organs, cells and tissues. Additionally, proper breathing:

Increases energy
Improves focus and concentration
Removes toxins
Fortifies the immune system
Improves bowel function
Reduces stress, tension and anxiety
Increases feelings of calmness and relaxation
Possibly lowers blood pressure
Increases metabolism to help digestion & weight loss

How to do it

- Lie on your back, stand up straight, or sit up straight in a chair.
- Place your hand on your belly, just below your ribs.
- Breathe normally.
- Does your upper chest rise? If so, you're breathing *improperly*.
- Does your hand on your belly rise? If so, you're breathing *properly*.

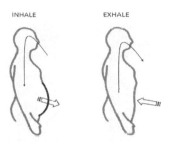

- Breathe in slowly and deeply, filling your lower belly so that it expands outward.
- Exhale slowly until your abdomen collapses inward.
- You can experiment with the count, but I suggest you start with counting slowly to yourself 1...2, as you inhale, and counting to yourself 1...2...3...4 as you exhale.

Note: Belly breathing is the technique you use with all of the meditation techniques in this book, and in all other books on meditation.

Trigger Word

Trigger word is a powerful tool that absolutely amazed me when I first began using it. It's actually pretty simple when you understand the process, and simple is always a good thing.

What a trigger word does

For our purposes, a trigger word functions like a start button to activate your subconscious into relaxing your mind and body anytime you want, wherever you want. By thinking or whispering your trigger word, you experience a mild sense of calm and relaxation sweep through your mind and body. The sensation isn't as profound as when you meditate for a few minutes, but it can be used to set the process in motion when you begin meditation or it can be used whenever you want to experience a pleasant sense of relaxation within seconds.

I've used my trigger word just before giving a presentation, before streaming out of a van to confront rioters, and on days when I felt especially anxious for no apparent reason.

I did a lot of media interviews during my years working street gangs. Because I never got used to being in front of the camera, I found that whispering or thinking my trigger word to myself a couple minutes before the camera's red light came on, helped to reduce my nervousness, helped me speak slowly and clearly, and made me look like I knew what I was talking about.

Here are a few ways you can use it:

- To bring on a mild sense of calm and relaxation during chaotic moments.
- To expedite the relaxation process when meditating.
- To deepen relaxation when meditating.
- To "recapture" calm and relaxation after being distracted from meditation.
- To facilitate regaining your composure after a traumatic incident.

Your trigger word

Choose any word(s) that you like, such as "calm," "relax," or "tension go." I use my middle name, "Wayne," because I use only my initial and I don't know anyone with that name. Plus, I can remember it.

Inputting your trigger word

To input your trigger word into your subconscious, you must use one of the meditation methods discussed in this book. It doesn't matter which one as long as it relaxes and calms you. Only when you're deeply relaxed are you susceptible to suggestions. The one in this case is this: *"Whenever I whisper or think my trigger word, I'll feel a profound sense of relaxation."*

You've been meditating for fifteen minutes using your favorite method and you're enjoying a wonderful sense of peace and tranquility. Take a few minutes to bask in those feelings and deepen them even more as you breathe slowly into your belly and exhale slowly.

Now it's time to input your trigger word. Whisper or think to yourself:

- *"Whenever I whisper or think my trigger word, I'll feel a profound sense of relaxation."*
- Say or think this about 10 times, with a few seconds between each.
  - o   Think about what you're saying each time.
  - o   Understand what you're saying each time.
- You might have to implant your word over several meditation sessions until it takes hold in your subconscious mind. If that's the case, it's okay; it's no big deal to do.

That's it. Pretty simple but amazingly effective.

How to use it when meditating

The trigger word is a good way to begin your meditation. Let's say you're going to meditate in your bedroom. It's been a crazy day and although you're home, you still feel as if you've just chugged three double espressos. It's time to get mellow.

Note: I'll remind you to return to this description whenever trigger word is mentioned in Section II, Meditation Methods.

Here is how you do it:

- Sit on a cushion, in a chair, or on the edge of your bed. Make sure your posture is straight and your hands are on your thighs, knees, or folded in your lap.
- Take a deep, slow breath into your lower belly, hold it for three or four seconds, and slowly release it. Repeat two or three more times.
- Now take in a deep breath, hold it, and slowly exhale as you whisper your trigger word.
- As you whisper it, mentally feel your body relax. Think of it as your muscles giving up the day's tensions and stressors.
- Whisper the word several times, and enjoy a sort of tingling sensation wash over your body, and your muscles soften and your mind begins to calm. That's the trigger working.
- Now begin whichever meditation method you like from Section 2 of this book and follow it to sink deeply into a quiet, calm, and relaxed state. Notice how you sink into it more quickly now that you've set the process in motion via your trigger word.

Many find that the trigger word expedites the relaxation as much as 20 to 30 percent. Think of it as a jumpstart to move you into that wonderful realm of calm and clarity a little quicker than if you hadn't used it at all.

Return to your trigger word should your meditation be somehow disrupted. Maybe you forgot to turn off your cell or someone came up and asked you something. If you had no choice but to answer your phone or answer the person's question, use your trigger word to return to that meditative place you were in prior to the interruption.

Use your trigger word anytime you want to bring on a mild sense of calm to better enjoy your day, to enhance your training progress, or to mellow yourself before a tough task.

Whispering or thinking your trigger word isn't going to relax you so much that you can't function on the job or train properly. Instead, it will give you better control over your mind and body.

SECTION II

INTRODUCTION
TO MEDITATION METHODS

Let's look at a variety of meditation methods that will serve you well as a martial artist, law enforcement officer, and soldier serving in a peaceful area or smack in the middle of a combat zone. Although you're presented with several methods here, you could easily get by with three or four and modify them depending on what you want to get out of your session.

You're also presented with several choices because one method doesn't serve everyone. While one Zen temple might teach only to follow the breath—in...out...in...out—another teaches a variety of methods and encourages people to find three or four that work best for them.

With some meditation methods, it takes only a minor adjustment to give yourself clarity of thought *before* an activity, to cool your adrenaline *after* a stressful situation, or to give yourself positive affirmations to better your performance *during* an activity. If you find one method for two or three purposes, that's great. If you need a different meditation method for each purpose, that's fine too. It's all about whatever works for you.

Can I do more than one method in one meditation session?

I asked the head monk of a Zen temple this question and he answered no, that it's best to choose one method and stick with it for your 5-, 10-, or 25-minute session. He said that when you focus on one and strive to be in the moment with it, you benefit even when it's not your favorite. In short, there is value using a method you dislike even when you think there isn't.

In Zen temples, meditators are taught not to judge a session. They learn to never say, "That was a bad sit. My monkey brain wouldn't calm down." This is because the benefit is in disciplining yourself to stay with it and keep returning your mind to stay in the moment. That is what makes you better and helps you grow.

Don't pass judgment too quickly. Sticking with a method you find difficult or think ineffective just might end up being your favorite. Keep in mind that some have been around for over 2,500 years. Some methods, such as following the breath, have been used by millions of meditators. Keep an open mind and a whole new world just might open to you.

Which methods don't I like?

One of the things I've learned as a martial arts instructor is to hold my tongue when it comes to giving an opinion on certain techniques. Over the years, there have been martial arts techniques that I thought were too complex or just plain silly to work in a street situation. For example, years ago, I taught that the spinning back kick was a dangerous lead move because you had to turn your entire body around—meaning your back was to the threat—to launch the leg. Then I met a black belt who could spin as fast as a tornado and never failed with it as a lead move.

I'm not going to prejudice you by saying which meditation methods I don't care for, or for that matter, which ones I like. Inevitably, you will hate my favorite ones and love those I don't like. I will, however, comment on any problems that might occur with a particular method and tell you how to fix them.

Being in the moment

As a fulltime writer, I have days when I sit down before the blank MAC screen at 8:30 and begin pounding the keys and, seemingly a short time later, look up at the clock expecting it to be 9:00 and find that it's 11:00.

Whether it's termed "total concentration," "mindfulness," or "being in the moment," it's definitely a powerful experience. Whenever you completely focus on something—writing, cleaning your weapon, kata movements, a tactical march—you push distractions aside and allow your mind to become refreshed and creative. As a result, it's more open to learning and better able to analyze, understand, and make decisions.

Conversely, when your mind is unfocused and bombarded with unnecessary thoughts, it's easily distracted, worried, and stressed. Mistakes come more easily too.

In this section, you will learn meditation methods for various purposes. The common thread that exists in all of them is to be in the moment. To facilitate that, all the methods require that you focus on your breathing. By concentrating on your breath—hearing and feeling the air pass through your nose, feeling it expand your belly, feeling the air leave your belly, feeling your belly contract, and feeling and hearing the air leave your mouth—allows your mind to be right here, right now, focused on one thing only.

This kind of single-point concentration liberates your mental processes and in time will benefit every aspect of your warrior life.

When you feel like stopping

Before we begin looking at meditation techniques, allow me a quick comment on quitting, something that every meditator has experienced. I learned this advice from something I read by Zen priest Susan O'Connell, Vice President on the Board of Directors at the San Francisco Zen Center. It's advice for meditators, but a technique you can apply to any number of your activities.

O'Connell says that when you're meditating and you feel like getting up—because you're bored, your leg is asleep, you're back is aching—don't do it. Just keep on meditating. Five or ten minutes later when you feel the urge to get up a second time, don't do it then, either. If after, say, another five minutes you feel another urge to quit…okay, you can stop then.

This means that you sit through the impulse to quit twice before finally giving in the third time. Taking this approach helps you develop the discipline to stay in your meditation longer and longer.

As a side note on the above paragraph, don't the words "give in" sound weak? Do you really want those to ever come out of your mouth? Meditate on that.

Key points:

Your mind will wander but don't let it bother you. Just gently bring it back on task.

- Meditate as long as you like, 5, 10, 15, or 25 minutes.
- You might think that meditation is making your mind even busier. In reality, you're merely becoming more aware of how busy it actually is

CHAPTER 4

MEDITATE TO ACHIEVE A POWERFUL SENSE OF CALM

To see a thing clearly in the mind makes it begin to take form ~ Henry Ford

I had been meditating for about two months when I ran into an old acquaintance I hadn't seen for a while. After chatting for a couple of minutes, he said, "There's something different about you. I can't quite put my finger on it but... I know what it is. You're so much calmer than the last time I saw you."

One of the first indicators I noticed after meditating for a short while was how mellow I was during the final days of wrapping a book. Some I've written in a few months and others have taken two to three years. However long it takes, there comes that day when I realize that I'm about to finish the project. No longer is finishing something that is going to happen in the future but rather something that is about to happen in a just a few days. This means I will be shipping it off to the publisher where numerous sets of eyes will look at my baby that I brought forth into the world—and pass judgment on it.

This can make those last few days of polishing and tweaking nerve wracking in the extreme. Before I meditated, I didn't sleep well the last week or so. I made silly writing mistakes, I was cranky, I was easily agitated, and I took it out on my cat, the dogs, and my family.

But after just a few weeks of almost daily meditation, which just coincidentally coincided with the end of a big book project, I noticed that I was cool, calm, and collected, even when my printer broke down and my PC ate several photos. I didn't curse or chew the insides of my mouth as I did in the past. Instead, I went about working calmly on fixing the problems. What a concept! Stay calm and fix things. That was a first for me and it felt wonderful.

Here are a few meditation methods that bring on a wonderful sense of calm, one that after a few weeks of practice stays with you.

Follow Your Breath Meditation

This is the meat-and-potatoes method used by many temples and monasteries. It's simple and it relies on only one tool, your breath. My breath? you say. What next, my hands? My feet? My butt? Well, yes. More on that later.

I used this method earlier this afternoon while waiting in line at the post office. Since I go four days a week, I decided a long time ago that I could either let my frustration over the interminably long lines drive me to throwing a flashbang into the lobby, or I could simply follow my breath. I chose the latter because I don't like the idea of going to jail and showering with tattooed prisoners.

So today, as I always do, I stood in line, focused my eyes on the tile floor, took a couple of deep breaths to relax me and set my meditation in motion, and then I simply followed my breath. Before I knew it, I had worked my way to the front of the line, and I was now calm, collected, and ready to buy stamps.

Here is how I did it. Notice that I follow the "set, sit, and forget" procedure that Dr. Storlie suggested earlier, except I did a "set, stand, and forget."

- I thought my trigger word three times to initiate the calming process. (See Chapter 3.)
- I took two or three deep breaths to settle my body and alert my brain as to what was happening.
- I told myself that I was going to follow my breath for a few minutes to bring on a nice sense of calm to my mind and body.
- I got comfortable in my standing position and looked totally natural doing so.

The above steps took about a minute to do.

- Dr. Storlie's third stage is to forget all your problems and to-do lists. I did, and I also tuned out the hubbub in the lobby. Was it easy? No, because distractions are, well, distracting. So when the woman behind me bumped my back, and the four-year-old banged her head into the counter and screamed bloody murder, I was briefly distracted. But I quickly acknowledged those things, let them go, and continued with my process.
- With my objective in place and my body and mind settled, I was ready to begin.
- I inhaled slowly, deeply, and quietly through my nose, and I mentally followed my breath's path to where it filled and expanded my lower belly.
- Then I followed my air back up through my chest and gently released it out of my mouth.

One inhalation and exhalation exchange took 10 to 15 seconds.

- I repeated this for the ten minutes it took to work my way to the front of the line. No one was the wiser, though if someone had been paying attention they might have noticed that I was the calmest person in the room.

Key points:

- Do the initial two or three deep breaths to ready your body and mind, and do them so quietly that if someone were standing next to you, they couldn't detect what you're doing.
- Feel your body grow progressively more relaxed on each exhalation of your initial two or three breaths.
- Breathe normally. It's common at first to breathe too quickly or too slowly. Just breathe at the same pace you always do.
- Breathe quietly.
- If your nose is plugged, inhale and exhale through your mouth.
- Breathe into your belly, not into your chest.

I once had the misfortune of sitting next to a guy at meditation session who, I'm convinced, thought he invented breathing. He inhaled so loudly that for a moment I wondered if he was trying to suck in everything and everyone around him. Then he blew it out so forcefully that it would have ruffled the guy's hair sitting 15 feet across from him if he hadn't been a bald-headed monk. There is no need to breathe like that. Breathe as quietly as you would if you were crawling through the dark to take out an enemy sentry.

Lori O'Connell, author of *When the Fight Goes to the Ground*, is a veteran jujitsu martial artist with multiple stripes on her tattered black belt. She follows a classic meditation method similar to how it's done in monasteries. She sits on a cushion right after getting up in the morning and meditates on the natural rhythm of her breath. Lori says:

"I just let myself be fully present in the moment and not let myself be too attached to the thoughts that go through my mind. Whatever thoughts do surface, I simply observe them, let them go, and return to focusing on my breath. Meditation helps me to remain calm and react better in aggressive situations. It helps me keep fear and anger in check and helps me to more clearly see what opportunities there are for avoidance, de-escalation, and combat."

4-Count Breathing Technique

This is sometimes called "Tactical breathing." It's an incredible calming meditation technique that is taught to police officers and military personnel as a fast way to slow the breathing, bring on a sense of calm, and even lower blood pressure. I know of police officers who have taught it quickly to citizens who were injured in traffic accidents and about to go into shock. Police and military snipers use it to calm themselves and still their hands before taking their shot.

One Army veteran of Afghanistan told me this:

> *"Every time I felt my heart start to race or my stress level rising, I used four-count breathing to calm myself. It became a potentially life-saving habit. Each time I did it, my thinking became more clear and, in some particularly dicey situations when my body wanted to freeze, it let me start moving again."*

There are three ways you can use 4-count breathing.

Variation 1: 4-count to quickly calm yourself

Let's say you're having a bad day and you're particularly agitated, nervous, upset, or tired. Use 4-count breathing to calm yourself, lower your blood pressure, and release tension from your body in less than five minutes.

Here is how you do it:

• Sit, lie, stand, or walk. (Standing and walking meditation are described in Chapter 6)
• Close your eyes all the way, close them partially, or leave them open. Whichever way works for you is what is important.
• To prepare your mind, inhale slowly and deeply, and exhale slowly. Repeat two or three more times.

Now you're ready to begin the 4-count.

• Breathe into your belly deeply and slowly through your nose to a count of four: 1, 2, 3, 4.
• Hold your breath in to a count of four: 1, 2, 3, 4.
• Slowly breathe out through your lips to a count of four: 1, 2, 3, 4.
• Hold it in to a count of four: 1, 2, 3, 4.
• Repeat two or three more times. More if you like.

Lt. Col. Dave Grossman and I wrote about this procedure in our book *On Combat*. We suggested that the agitated warrior do three cycles to bring on a quick calming effect. We recommended this number for two reasons. First, in an ongoing stressful event there might not be time to do more. Secondly, anecdotal reports suggest that three exchanges seem to calm most people. Can you do more? Yes. You can do as many as you like.

Although 4-count seems to be popular, you can increase it to 5-count, or 6-count if you like. That means you will breathe in to a count of 5 or 6, hold for a count of 5 or 6, exhale for a count of 5 or 6, and hold it for a count of 5 or 6.

Variation 2: 4-count as a lead-in to your meditation

Use the 4-count method as a way to calm and relax yourself quickly before you begin doing whatever meditative technique you choose.

Here is how to do it:

- Sit, lie, stand, or walk. (Standing and walking meditation are described in Chapter 6)
- Close your eyes all the way, close them partially, or leave them open.
- To prepare your mind, inhale slowly and deeply, and exhale slowly. Repeat two or three more times.
- Inhale to the count of 4 as you feel and "see" your breath enter through your nose and travel through your lungs to fill your belly. It might be helpful to imagine your breath to be a color. Many people use aqua blue since it connotes coolness and calming.
- Hold the breath in your belly to the count of 4 as you feel and see the air churning and tumbling about.
- Exhale the air to the count of 4, as you feel and see the air exit your belly, travel upward through your torso and out your mouth.
- Hold your belly empty to a count of 4, as you feel and see the emptiness in your belly.
- If you want to do two or three more cycles before you begin your meditation, that's fine.
- When you're ready, proceed to the meditation method of your choice.

Variation 3: 4-count as your sole meditation method

This is a little different than Variation 1: "4-count to quickly calm yourself," in that in this case it's done longer. When used to calm yourself, it's generally done for three of four cycles, which takes about three minutes. But when used as your sole meditation method, you continue through the cycles for 5, 10, up to 25 minutes.

Here is how to do it:

- Sit, lie, stand, or walk. (Standing and walking meditation are described in Chapter 6)
- Close your eyes all the way, close them partially, or leave them open.
- To prepare your mind, inhale slowly and deeply, and exhale slowly. Repeat two or three more times.
- Now proceed through the 4-count steps for as long as you want.

Veteran martial artist Jerry Fulford meditates daily, often several times a day, following 4-count breathing. He says:

[It's about] *"an awareness on the breathing. The goal is for the mind not to be occupied by a thousand random thoughts. You simply sit in a chair (easy to do for us westerners). Sit on the front edge and keep your spine erect. This helps you not fall asleep and allows you to sit for long periods.*

"In the early stages, I recommend setting a timer for 5 minutes with a goal of maintaining awareness for that period. You then increase the time as needed. I do 30 minutes every day now, and longer sessions when I'm on

my days off and on vacation. I think it's most beneficial to do random meditative moments throughout the day. These help with your focus and give you a boost of energy and clarity throughout.

"My objective is to attain all the health benefits research has found in meditation, as well as to control my thoughts and enjoy moments of pure relaxing quietness.

"I mainly meditate while sitting, and sometimes while running or walking. My main practice is to sit in the morning, but at this stage, I do it often and throughout the day.

I have found that once you control your mind (single focus), everything becomes meditation.

"As far as meditation enhancing my learning ability, retention, performance in class, competition and awareness on the street, it has helped me a lot. Decreasing my stress is the biggest benefit—I'm a former hot head— I'm able to concentrate more, I think things through now instead of overreacting, I have lots more energy, and I achieve my goals more easily.

"Mental training plays a large role in any activity, and if you don't train your mind, you miss out on better performance overall."

A veteran of the Afghanistan war found what many other returning troops have discovered. He said:

"Back home, I use four-count breathing to counteract anxiety issues that are souvenirs from my time overseas. When I feel overwhelmed or I feel a panic attack coming on, I close my eyes, breathe in, hold it in, release it, and hold empty, all for a four (sometimes longer) count."

Key points:

- Count to 4 at a moderate pace in the time it would take you add the words, "one thousand" before each number. For example: One thousand one, one thousand two… Don't rush it and don't go too slowly.

Touch And Sound Meditation

It doesn't matter where you do this. It can even be in a packed baseball stadium, on a stakeout, or on a crowed bus. No one will know what you're doing or even notice you.

As the name suggests, this method is about focusing your attention on your sense of touch and hearing. For example, say you're going to begin by focusing on your hands. It doesn't matter where they are: resting on your knees, in your coat pockets, clasped in your lap, or holding a piece of equipment. After 30 seconds, move your attention to one singular sound that you hear. You might hear lots—traffic, police radio, an instructor calling cadence, someone working on the heavy bag—but you are to focus on just one.

Here is how to do this simple procedure:

You can use your trigger word to get started or, since we just discussed the 4-count breathing technique, let's use it.

- Sit, lie, stand, or walk. (Standing and walking meditation are described in Chapter 6)
- Close your eyes all the way, close them partially, or leave them open.
- To prepare your mind, inhale slowly and deeply, and exhale slowly. Repeat two or three more times.
- To prepare: Breathe slowly and deeply into your lower belly to the count of 4, 1-2-3-4. Hold it in to a count of 4, 1-2-3-4. Exhale slowly to a count of 4, 1-2-3-4. Hold empty for a count of 4, 1-2-3-4. Focus your mind on your breaths. Do this 4-part exchange two or three

more times. This relaxes you and prepares you for the meditation.

• Touch: Focus now on what your hands are touching. (Be aware without moving them.)

    o   Notice their warmth, roughness, softness, and the bones. If your hands are resting on your thighs or knees, feel the texture of the cloth or bare skin, the warmth or the coolness. If they are in your pockets, feel the material and the warmth.

    o   Put all your awareness on this contact point but don't pass judgment on it. If the surface is rough, be aware of it but don't judge it as good or bad. If you have a sore finger, don't judge it as bad.

    o   Should your mind wander, just bring it back to the moment and that place where your hands touch.

    o   After 30 seconds—60 if you're an experienced meditator—slowly transition your mind to a sound.

• Sound: Let's make it the sound of passing traffic. Hear it but don't judge it. Hear the hum, the passing diesel truck, the motorcycle, and the siren. Don't think—*that's a garbage truck, that's got to be a Honda motorcycle,* or *there must be a fire close by*. Just experience the sound. After 30 seconds—60 if you're an experienced meditator—slowly transition your mind back to your hands and what you feel.

• Touch: Repeat the 30- or 60-second procedure as described above.

• Sound: Repeat the 30- or 60-second procedure as described above.

Key Points:

- Continue moving your mind from your hands to the sound and back to your hands again.
- When a thought bubbles to the surface of your mind—*I'm hungry; I need to gas up my truck; the big game is on tonight*—just let the thought go and return your mind to the sound or the feel of your hands.
- Your hands, your rear, and whatever you're sitting on, or the feel of your feet on the floor, are popular focus targets because they are always present. Just as is sound.
- If at first you don't de-stress a little from this simple meditation, don't give up. You will.
- It's all about focusing your thoughts, being in the moment and, ultimately, releasing your stress.

Counting Breaths Meditation

As the name implies, you will simply count your inhalations and your exhalations, a technique that has been popular among meditators for millenniums.

Here is how you do it:

- Sit, lie, stand, or walk. (Standing and walking meditation are described in Chapter 6)
- Close your eyes all the way, close them partially, or leave them open.
- To prepare your mind, inhale slowly and deeply, then exhale slowly. Repeat two or three more times.
- As you breathe in, think "one" in your mind.
- As you exhale, think "two" in your mind.
- Typically, people count to 10, but if at first you encounter lots of distractions, don't try to count that high. Instead, count to 4 and then start over at one. When that's easy, bump it up to 6, then 8 and then— voila!—10.
- Once you're able to count 10 breaths—5 inhalations and 5 exhalations—count backward to 1. So after you inhale on 9 and exhale on 10, begin to count backward by inhaling and thinking "10" and exhaling and thinking "9." When you can count from 1 to 10 with minimum distraction and from 10 to 1, also with minimum distraction, you're on your way to mastery.

Key Points:

- Even if you have mastered this method, there might be days when you have trouble reaching 10. When that happens, don't worry about it. Simply return to counting to 4 or 5. Don't judge and don't fret. Do what you can do.
- If you're more of a sound person, you will "hear" the number in your head. If you're a visual person, you will "see" the number in your mind as "One" or "1." Some people like to see the "one" or "1" emerge out of the darkness, disappear, then see "two" or "2" emerge and disappear.
- If you find it easy to stay focused, then count "one" or "1" for both the inhalation and the exhalation. If you're visual, see the "one' or "1" as you inhale and continue to see it until you exhale. If you like to hear the number, do so in your head as you inhale and hear it again as you exhale. So by the time you reach 10, you have done 10 complete breath exchanges.
- Go at whatever pace is comfortable. There is never a rush to progress.

My New Zealand friend, Bryan Ward, an aikido practitioner and senior constable, has been meditating for years.

"I find that combined with my aikido practice, meditating helps me to be a lot calmer than most people, and I'm able to relax a lot more around friends and family after hours.

"I sit in seiza [sits on his knees, his rear on his heels], and breathe through my nose and out my mouth, counting my breaths. I try to control my thoughts but after about six years of practice, I am yet to make it to 6 breaths. That said, once a thought comes into my mind, I allow it to

*happen and move on back to the breathing without being
hung up on the thought."*

Note: It's the act of continually returning to your meditation
that is so critical. That's what makes you a disciplined
meditator and what improves your ability over time. Don't
get frustrated and never give up.

Erratic Breathing Meditation

A few years ago after meditating for a long while, I suddenly couldn't focus. I'd count the first inhalation and exhalation, and when I should have been counting the next one, I was thinking about punching the heavy bag. I couldn't get out of this easily distracted pattern and my loud cursing was disturbing the other meditators. I'm kidding about the cursing, but I did switch to this simple technique that quickly got me back on course.

Here is how to do it:

- Sit, stand, lie, or walk. (Standing and walking meditation are described in Chapter 6)
- Close your eyes all the way, close them partially, or leave them open.
- To prepare your mind, inhale slowly and deeply, then exhale slowly. Repeat two or three more times.

Now you're ready to begin erratic breathing.

- Breathe in slowly using two or three short inhalations without exhaling.
- Hold it in for five seconds.
- Then exhale slowly using two or three short exhalations.
- Repeat for four or five exchanges.
- Now inhale in one long breath and one short breath.
- Don't hold it in this time, but exhale it in one long breath and one short one.
- Repeat for four or five exchanges.
- Do this for as long as you like, 2 minutes, 5 minutes, 10, 15, or longer.

Key Points:

• The two erratic breathing methods above are just two ways to break up your inhalation and exhalation. There are many, such as inhaling in four short breaths and exhaling in one long one. Or inhaling in one long breath and exhaling in five short ones. Simply use your imagination to vary the pattern. Just don't hyperventilate.

• You can change the pattern on every inhalation and exhalation, or repeat a method four or five times before changing to a different one.

• You can breathe erratically for your entire session or for just a few minutes until you feel that you're focused and ready to breathe normally.

Sound Meditation

One warrior meditator said that she thinks of herself as a symphony conductor and all the sounds in her world are her orchestra. Here are several ways to meditate to sound.

Merging sounds

Tom Levak is an old friend of mine who began studying karate in 1964, one year before me. Over the years he has won 18 national championships, two AAU National Championships, and approximately 15 international and world championships, some of those while competing in his 60s against 18 year olds. He recently placed second in a tournament at the age of 74. Here is what he says about meditating to sound.

"I practice what I call 'listening meditation.' I relax, usually reclining, and focus my mind on all outside sounds at the same time. Whatever sounds I hear—birds chirping, passing cars, a running stream, everything—I merge together but without thinking about them. I find that this kind of focus eliminates thoughts and calms my entire body and refreshes my spirit."

How to do it.

- Sit, stand, lie, or walk. (Standing and walking meditation are described in Chapter 6)
- Close your eyes all the way, close them partially, or leave them open.
- To prepare your mind, inhale slowly and deeply, and exhale slowly. Repeat two or three more times.
- Become aware of all the surrounding sounds, no matter how loud or soft.
- Now unite all these sounds so that you hear all of them as just one,.
- Should your mind extract one sound—a ticking clock, an overhead jet—simply merge it back with all the others.
- Do this for as long as you like, 2 minutes, 5, 10, 15, or longer.

Separating sounds meditation

Lisa Place is my partner in life, a hard training martial artist with two black belts in two fighting arts, an axe thrower, and an archer. She is also a long-time meditator. She likes to meditate to sound but her approach is the exact opposite of Tom Levak's. She says:

"I like to separate the sounds, acknowledge one, and move on to the next. For example, first I'm aware of the sound of my breathing. I acknowledge it as mine, and then move to the sound of an overhead jet, acknowledge what it is, and move on to the sound of my cat purring. I don't think about these sounds, such as my stuffy nose, or how I wish I were on that jet going to Hawaii. Instead, I

simply recognize them for what they are. This recognition takes only a second or two, and then I move on. I find that this simple process relaxes me and keeps me focused in the moment."

How to do it.

- Sit, stand, lie, or walk. (Standing and walking meditation are described in Chapter 6)
- Close your eyes all the way, close them partially, or leave them open.
- To prepare your mind, inhale slowly and deeply, and exhale slowly. Repeat two or three more times.
- Become aware of all the surrounding sounds, no matter how loud or soft.
- Pick one sound.
- Acknowledge it for what it is—*that's a truck, that's a lawnmower*—and move on to the next sound.
- If the only sounds you can hear are your breathing, dripping water from a roof gutter, and an occasional jet, move from the first one, to the second, to the third, and back to the first one again.
- Do this for as long as you like, 5 minutes, 10, 15, or longer.

Following a sound meditation

This is another one of Lisa's. Here is what she says about it:

"Sometimes I follow one single sound. If a car passes, I'll follow it in my mind until I no longer hear it. Same with an airplane overhead. When I used to sit in a Zen temple, I would follow the sound of late arrivals. I'd hear their soft footsteps, the swishing of their clothes, and I'd listen until they sat down. I didn't wonder what kind of a

car it was, or imagine where the plane was going, or try to guess who the late arrival was. I'd simply acknowledge the sound and follow it until it no long existed."

How to do it

- Sit, stand, lie or walk. (Standing and walking meditation are described in Chapter 6)
- Close your eyes all the way, close them partially, or open them.
- To prepare your mind, inhale slowly and deeply, and exhale slowly. Repeat two or three more times.
- Become aware of all the surrounding sounds, no matter how loud or soft.
- Pick one sound and focus on it.
- If the sound is mobile—someone walking by, a passing car, an airplane—follow it until you no longer hear it. Then pick another sound.
- If the sound is constant—dripping water, fan, freeway, ocean surf—focus on it as long as you like. Don't judge it as good or bad or think about what it is, just listen.

Melting Face Meditation

I gave this method its cool name. I've done it for years, enjoying the way I feel during and after my session. I sometimes go so deeply with it that it's hard to move when I've finished. I just want to remain in the ultra peaceful zone forever.

I had an outside hot tub for several years. I remember sitting in it so many times late at night after a rough work shift, and scooting down in the 104-degree water so that only my nose and eyes were above the surface (sort of like a gator). I fell asleep a few times, slipping peacefully under the water, only to wake up with a lot of sputtering and hard coughing. But those times when I didn't nearly drown and I knew it was time to get out, it could be almost impossible to do. While one part of my brain told me I'd been in the hot water too long, another part, as well as my body, were arguing against it, and grumbling and whining when I finally managed to stand and step out of that place of profound relaxation and calm. The same thing often happens when doing "Melting Face Meditation."

(One meditator said he thinks about how the bad guys' faces melted at the end of the movie, *Raiders of the Lost Ark*. Hey, whatever works.)

Here is how you do it.

• Sit, stand, lie or walk. (Standing and walking meditation are described in Chapter 6)
• Close your eyes all the way, close them partially, or open them.
• Whisper or think your trigger word three or four times.
• To prepare your mind, inhale slowly and deeply, and exhale slowly. Repeat two or three more times.
• Take a moment to become aware of your face
• Begin by focusing on your forehead. Inhale slowly, and as you gently exhale think or say to yourself in a soft whisper, *melt*. Say it two or three times if you want. Each time you think or say this word, feel your forehead become relaxed, heavy, as if melting off your skull, like wax down a candle. Repeat as many times as you like.
• Focus on your eyebrows and eyes. Inhale slowly, and then as you exhale think or say to yourself in a soft whisper, *melt*. Say it two or three times if you want. Each time you think or say this, feel your eyebrows and eyes become relaxed and heavy. Do as many breath exchanges needed to feel these facial features melting in total relaxation.
• Focus on your nose and cheekbones. Inhale slowly, and as you exhale slowly think or say to yourself in a soft whisper, *melt*. Say it two or three times if you want. Each time you think or say this, feel your nose and cheekbones become relaxed and heavy, as if melting off your skull like wax oozing down a candle.
• Pause here for a moment. Before you move down to your mouth and chin, evaluate the state of your relaxation thus far. If you need to do a few breath exchanges and *melt* commands to reestablish deep relaxation in your forehead, eyebrows, eyes, nose, or cheeks before moving on, do it now. And always remember, there is no rush. Take your time. Enjoy the process.

• Focus on your mouth and jaw. If this is a tension point for you, this will feel especially wonderful. Inhale slowly, and as you exhale think or say to yourself in a soft whisper, *melt*. Say it two or three times if you want. Each time you think or say this, feel your mouth and jaw become relaxed and heavy, as if melting off your skull.

• Focus on your neck. Inhale slowly and as you exhale slowly think or say to yourself in a soft whisper, *melt*. Say it two or three times if you want. Each time you think or say this, feel your neck, all four sides, become relaxed and heavy. Repeat as many times as you like.

That's as far down as you go. Now for the next few minutes, spot-check your face and melt any part that needs a little extra. Should you want to start over because you're enjoying it so much, do it. Sometimes the melting sensation extends a while after you quit meditating for the day. It doesn't always, darn-it, but when it does it's an extra bonus.

Key points:

• Feel free to break the steps down further. For example, instead of melting your eyebrows and eyes together, do them separately. First melt your eyebrows and once you've got them dripping, melt your eyes. Melt your right cheek first and then melt your left.

• As always, if a thought wanders in, acknowledge it, and go back to your melting. It will go away on its own.

• Think: "liiiim melllltiiiing!"

CHAPTER 5

MEDITATE TO PREPARE FOR TRAINING

If you realized how powerful your thoughts are, you would never think a negative thought again – anon

Let's begin with a brief explanation as to how your brain works and how using affirmations and mental imagery in your meditation will dramatically help you get more out of your training.

Your conscious mind

This is the logical, thinking part of your brain, the part that knows how to strip a weapon, understand the meaning of kata, and knows how to read suspicious people. A conscious wide-awake mind is in beta state (see Chapter 2 for an explanation of beta and alpha waves).

Your subconscious mind

Your subconscious makes associations between things and people, and determines how it will react to them. It contains apprehension, desire, anxiety, habits, and your many personality traits.

You can change these things in your subconscious, but first you have to get by your conscious mind to do so. The problem is that when you're awake, your conscious mind works hard to keep you from accessing it. However, there is a way around this. If you guessed meditation, you're right.

Your subconscious is highly susceptible to suggestions just before falling asleep, right after waking up, and when you're relaxed through meditation. Because it cannot distinguish between reality and fantasy (suggestions), the subconscious can be successfully re-programmed with affirmations and mental imagery.

Affirmations

Negative thinking

Most often, people use negative words and statements about themselves, and the situation they're in or about to confront. No doubt you have heard people say: "I just don't shoot well at the 50-yard line." "I will never get better at sparring." "I just can't get this criminal law stuff." By repeating such statements to themselves and to others, they imprint these negatives into their heads so that their conscious minds guide them to shoot poorly, to not improve at sparring, and to not learn criminal law. And here is the especially scary part. If you're guilty of this, know that the more you repeat these negatives, the deeper they're gouged into your subconscious brain.

The simple fact is that repeated words and statements have a powerful effect on your subconscious mind, whether negative or positive. Consequently, they can either destroy or build you up. Here is a bumper sticker from Henry Ford:

"Whether you think you can or you can't, you're right."

Positive thinking

Consider these six bullets:

- Affirmations are positive words and statements that set into motion a desired result.
- When repeated often, they become imprinted on your subconscious mind *over* the negative imprints you've established there.
- The positive affirmations guide your actions to the desired result you want.
- To ensure the effectiveness of the affirmations, you must repeat them with your full attention, and with faith and desire for the positive outcome.
- Meditation is the best way to do the imprinting.
- By calming your mind, you're able to reach your subconscious and begin changing all the negativity that has been ingrained there.

How long does it take to calm the mind to be receptive?

How long depends on the individual and a host of other factors. For now, let's use 20 minutes as a baseline, which is generally sufficient time to calm your mind and body. With experience, it can take you less than 20 minutes.

If for whatever reason you don't feel calm and relaxed after 20 minutes—you've had an insanely hectic day, you were interrupted during the 20 minutes meditation, you're new to the process—go ahead and do the affirmations anyway. You still benefit to some degree and it will get you in the groove of doing the procedure.

As mentioned, it won't always take this long. Most find that after a while they're able to induce a calm, receptive state after, say, five or ten minutes. I mention this at the risk of making the process sound like a drive-up fast food joint, which isn't the case at all. Twenty minutes is better; five minutes is minimum no matter how good you get at it.

Affirmations Before Training

I was taking private tai chi lessons when I first discovered the power of preparing the mind for training. Tai chi is a type of martial art that originated in China and has become immensely popular in the United States and other non-Asian countries. It's generally thought of as "that Chinese exercise where people move very sloooowly." While it is that, it's also a viable fighting art that has stood the test of time. (It should be mentioned that when used for self-defense the movements are done fast. Someone always asks).

At the time, I had been training for a long time in the fighting arts, but I found the precision and rhythmic flow of tai chi a little difficult to do since my fighting style at that time was similar to a charging locomotive.

One day, I got to class about 15 minutes early. It had been a busy and crazy morning, so I welcomed the time to make myself comfortable in my car and take a few deep breaths to center myself before following my breath. Once I felt deeply relaxed, I told myself that:

- I was calm.
- I was in control of my thoughts and my body.
- I would be receptive to my teacher's instruction.

I repeated these three commands several times. When it was time to go into class, I was happily mellow, in command of my thoughts and muscles, and ready for whatever complex moves my teacher had in store.

I subsequently did this meditation whenever time allowed, finding that the simple procedure dramatically helped my receptiveness to my instructor's lessons and to ultimately learn this art that was new to me.

Conversely, on those occasions when my mornings were crazy and I rushed to class with only seconds to spare, and thus no time to meditate and give myself suggestions, I wasn't as receptive and my performance wasn't up to par.

Here is how to do it:

- Sit, stand, lie or walk. (Standing and walking meditation are described in Chapter 6)
- Close your eyes all the way, close them partially, or open them.
- To prepare your mind, inhale slowly and deeply, and exhale slowly. Repeat two or three more times.
- If you have 20 minutes before you train, take at least 5 minutes to focus on your breathing to bring on a sense of calm and quiet. You can also use your trigger word or 4-count tactical breathing to facilitate the process.
- Each time you exhale, feel your head and body relax more and more. Think the words *calm, relax, or melt* on each slow exhalation.
- Once you feel calm and quiet, think or whisper aloud the following positive words:

"I am calm and receptive to learning."
"I'm dedicated to improving."
"I'm focused on improving."
"My mind is on the task."
"My mind is in the moment."
"I am excited to get started."
"I'm an easy learner."
"The training is easy for me."
"I'm listening to the instructor and following directions."
"I'm good and I'm getting better each training session."

Key points:

- Tailor the above to fit your situation.
- Important: Don't state your affirmations in the negative. Don't say: "The training is not hard for me." Make your affirmations positive: "Training is easy for me."
- Keep your affirmations in the present. Say, "I'm listening to the instructor and following directions" even if your training doesn't take place for several hours.

Mental Imagery

Tactical mental imagery before your training

Tactical imagery is sometimes erroneously called "visualization." The problem with this word is that it implies that you only "see" the training exercises in your mind. In reality, however, you use *all of your senses* when training. Therefore, it's better to engage—to image—as many of your senses as you can.

In your mind's eye, image:

- what you would *see*.
- what you would *hear*.
- what you would *feel* (physically and emotionally).
- what you would *smell*.
- what you would *taste*.

The more intense and realistic your imagery the greater your results in reality. Don't rush through this. Clearly and vividly:

- *see* your training partner's incoming kick.
- *feel* your weapon firing round after round.
- *smell* and *taste* the gun smoke.
- *hear* your instructor's command.
- *feel* your enthusiasm for the drill.
- *feel* any fear you have.
- *feel* and *see* yourself function through your fear.

Here is how to do use meditation to image a simple self-defense move against a knife slash:

- Sit, stand, lie or walk. (Standing and walking meditation are described in Chapter 6)
- Close your eyes all the way, close them partially, or open them.
- To prepare your mind, inhale slowly and deeply, and exhale slowly. Repeat two or three more times.
- If you have 20 minutes before you train, take at least 5 minutes to focus on your breathing to bring on a sense of calm and quiet.
- Each time you exhale, feel your head and body relax more and more. Think the words *calm, relax, or melt* on each slow exhalation.

Once you feel calm and quiet, you're ready to image your defense against a knife assault.

- *See* yourself in the parking area of a strip mall.
- *Hear* traffic out on the street, and *hear* and *see* people coming and going.
- *Feel* the warmth of the summer day and the hardness of the sidewalk on which you're standing.
- *See* the armed man clearly in your mind i.e., he's wearing a red polo shirt, blue jeans, blue running shoes, and he's gripping a knife with a six-inch blade. The blade is in his right hand and he's slashing it from right to left.
- *Hear* his verbal threat: "I'm going to cut you up and watch you bleed out."
- *Feel* adrenaline surge through your muscles, especially your legs and arms.
- *Feel* your heart rate and your breathing increase.
- *Feel* a sense of control flow through your body.

Because you're jammed between a red vehicle and a white one, you have no option but to lunge into the arc of the blade.

- *Feel* your leg muscles thrust.
- *Feel* and *see* your two arms thrust forward to block his inner forearm.
- *Hear* the two of you grunt as your arms slam into his.
- *Feel* your hands grab his arm with your hands.
- *Feel* the cloth of his shirt
- *See* the knife dangerously close to your abdomen.
- *Feel* your legs drive him backwards until his arm strikes the side of a black Honda.
- *Feel* your knee slam into his groin over and over.
- *Hear* his grunts turn to screams.
- *See* him begin to slouch from the pain of your blows.
- *Feel* your arm slam his arm into the edge of the car hood repeatedly until the knife drops from his hand.
- *See* and *feel* your foot kick the knife under the car.
- *See* and *feel* your hands roll him onto his belly and secure his arm in a painful control hold.
- *Hear* the warm round of applause from the onlookers. (Hey, it's your imagery. Be a hero in it.)

A variation using small movement

While mental imagery is done in your mind, know that you don't have to always sit perfectly still when practicing. From time to time use mini movements that mimic what you're imaging. Don't move at full speed, full force, or with full extension of your limbs. Don't even move at half or quarter speed. Just move ever so slightly, slowly, and gently.

Watch Olympic athletes before they launch themselves down a snowy ski slope or jump up onto gymnastic high bars. Many of them—some with their eyes closed, some with them open—make very small movements with their heads and arms.

Let's say you want to image the above self-defense against a knife slash scenario while lying down or sitting in a chair. Simply close your eyes and see, hear, feel, smell, and even taste the situation unfold as your arms, head, torso, and legs move ever so minimally.

Don't do this in line at the grocery.

Before you get out of bed imagery

If it's awkward time-wise and location-wise for you to meditate right before a training session, here is a simple, short, and effective meditation that that you can do while you're still mellow from sleeping, a time when your subconscious is already somewhat receptive to suggestions. It's effective even when your training is scheduled for later in the day.

It takes only 5 or 10 minutes, though you can certainly do it longer if you so choose. It's common to hear people say that their initial intentions were to meditate for only 5 minutes, but after a few sessions they increased the time because they enjoyed the process and gained much more than they ever imagined. But if you're new to it, 5 to 10 minutes will reward you with tremendous benefits.

Set the alarm for 10 minutes in case you fall back to sleep.

Here is how to do it.

- Remain in bed, and either close your eyes all the way, close them partially, or keep them open. Rest your arms along your sides.

• To prepare your mind, inhale slowly and deeply, and exhale slowly. Repeat two or three more times.
• Remember, to fully relax you must breathe into your belly, not into your chest. If it helps, rest your hand on your chest at first to ensure it doesn't rise on your inhalation.
• Breathe in through your nose and deliberately push your belly outward as you fill your lungs. When you exhale, release the air from your belly out through your nose or mouth.
• Repeat this process until you feel calm.

Imagery

• *See* your training environment clearly in your mind, imaging as much detail as you can.
• *Feel* the ground, the training mat, or the floor of the indoor shooting range.
• *Smell* the odors associated with the environment: the stuffy gym, the pine forest, or the fresh paint on the walls.
• *Hear* the sounds associated with your training: grunts, gunshots, thumps on the heavy bag, sirens.
• Using all of your senses, image yourself participating in the training.
• *See* and *hear* yourself listening to the instructions, following them, and performing at your best.
• *Feel* yourself full of confidence, energy, and enthusiasm.
• *Feel* yourself learning and progressing.
• *See* yourself finishing the session and *feel* yourself happy with your training.

Key points:

- Keep your imagery positive. Don't think of mistakes you've made before or think about how much you dislike the training or the trainer. Image yourself learning, enjoying, and progressing.
- Use all your senses, including your taste.
- Know that the process, both the relaxation phase and the imagery phase, gets easier each time you do it.

Meditation Imagery To Psyche Up For Your Training

I used to compete in martial arts tournaments with a pair of Japanese sickles called *kama*. No, I didn't compete against a live opponent because the bloodshed would have been worse than a Quentin Tarantino movie. I entered the kata competition, performing a 100-movement "battle" against invisible multiple opponents.

Kata competitors are judged on precision of movement, grace, speed, power, and warrior spirit. In time, I felt confident in my physical ability, but I wanted to bring a sense of real battle to my performance. So I developed a form of imagery meditation in which I would psyche myself mentally and charge my body physically into believing that I was a fierce warrior as I whirled and slashed and hacked with my sickles.

As soon as the ring judges assigned the competitors their position in the line-up to perform, I would go off by myself and begin to meditate. I didn't sit down nor did I stand still. Instead, I paced. While holding a sickle in each hand and with my eyes semi closed, I would stride back and forth— half a dozen steps forward and half a dozen steps back—all the while I imaged myself a *ronin* samurai hired to protect a small Japanese village from invaders at the foot of Mt. Fuji. Hey, don't laugh. It worked and it worked great. Of course, I had seen so many samurai movies that it was easy to image stomping around the dusty village streets with my topknot, sickles, and bad attitude.

Sometimes I had 15 minutes to meditate and other times I had only five. In either case, I would deliberately increase my breathing rate, tense and relax my muscles, and make mini motions with my sickles. By the time my name was called to compete, my breathing had actually accelerated, I was sweating as if I'd already performed, and I was of a mindset that I was ready to wipe out any and all invaders.

Did it help? Yes. I won first or placed in the top three positions in over 50 tournaments. Other competitors and people from the audience commented on the ferocity I brought to the competition, and some even said that that I looked like an enraged samurai. (My favorite compliment came from a buddy who said that with my greying hair and beard, I looked like a really, really mad Kenny Rogers.)

I also used a similar method to psyche myself before going on a police raid, before serving a warrant on an especially dangerous wanted person, and before a rigorous police training session. As will be discussed in a moment, sometimes I had to fake the psyche, and that's okay. Even when faking, it can still work. Fake it till you make it, goes the saying.

Here is one way to psyche yourself before a training session:

- Sit, stand, lie or walk. (Standing and walking meditation are described in Chapter 6)
- Close your eyes all the way, close them partially, or open them.
- To prepare your mind, inhale slowly and deeply, and exhale slowly. Repeat two or three more times.
- Follow your breath for a few minutes, or use any other meditation method you like, to bring on a sense of calm and clarity to ready your mind for the imagery.

Now you're ready to use imagery to psyche yourself ready.

- *See* the training area: martial arts school, shooting range, obstacle course, mock city, etc.
- *See* yourself on site ready to participate in the exercises.
- *Feel* your energy and anticipation surge through your body.
- *Feel* your chest expand as you deliberately increase your breathing rate.
- *Feel* fresh adrenaline charge your muscles.
- *Feel* and *see* your fists open and close a few times as the energy floods your body.
- *See* and *feel* your body:
    o launch powerful backfists.
    o strategically enter a room.
    o search and handcuff a training partner.
    o fire a weapon.
    o execute a mock felony car stop.
- *Feel* your every cell fill with adrenaline, anticipation, desire, enthusiasm, and hardcore psych.
- *Feel* and *see* yourself performing flawlessly.

Key points:

- What if you don't feel the energy, enthusiasm, or excitement? Then fake until you do. Draw on the last time you felt excited and hard charged about doing something and bring that to your meditation.
- Know that "Fake it till you make it" is much more than a cute phrase or New Age doublespeak.
  - Aristotle said, "Acting virtuous will make one virtuous."
  - Therapists recommend to patients suffering from depression that they act like they are enjoying their daily activities, though it might feel forced at first. In time, many patients find that after a while they do indeed feel happy.
  - Fake it with all the realism you can bring to it and you will be amazed at how quickly you really do feel psyched and ready to go.

During my competition years, I was often terrified to compete in front of hundreds of people against other veteran martial artists. But by first imagining myself getting worked up into a hard-charging warrior samurai, I not only overcame my fear, but in time I was able to infuse my mind and body with a fiery warrior spirit.

Meditating On An Issue

Earlier, I mentioned that meditating on an issue is a powerful tool that allows you to see all sides of it. By first entering into a deep meditative state, your calm and focused mind allows you to examine more intensely than you normally do. I'm fairly used to it now, but when I began meditating on various issues a few years ago, I was amazed at how much was revealed.

Here is how you do it:

- Decide what you want to meditate on. Let's say that you would like to be more aggressive.
    - As a cop it might be a weakness in how you approach a suspect.
    - As a soldier, it might be your approach to an indigenous person.
    - As a martial artist, it might be your reluctance to go on the offensive.
- Sit, stand, lie or walk. (Standing and walking meditation are described in Chapter 6)
- Close your eyes all the way, close them partially, or open them.
- Whisper or think your trigger word three or four times.

Choose a meditation method to sink deeply into a quiet, calm, and relaxed state.

- When you're ready, consider the issue as it affects you.
- Can you see anything in your past that might be the cause?
    - o   If so, analyze it, break it down, and look at it from all sides.
- Has there been one recent experience that affected you?
    - o   If so, analyze it, break it down, and look at it from all sides.
    - o   Can you see where your response had a negative result and thus a lasting affect on you?
- Examine your strengths to see how they might offer a solution.
    - o   Can your strength in one area bring up the weakness in another?
    - o   How would you do that?
- In what ways can you fake being aggressive until it becomes part of you?
    - o   Are there any drawbacks?

You get the idea. You continue to ask yourself questions, offer suggestions, and make observations, as you look at all sides of the issue. If you don't find a solid solution the first time you meditate on something, do it again next time. Each successive time, you're entering the meditation with more information derived from your last session.

It's a powerful tool, one that you get better at each time out. It's also an enjoyable experience in which you learn about yourself.

Key points:

- Meditate on only one issue at a time.
- Don't discount anything that arises in your mind, no matter what it is. Give it a look. If you're ultimately convinced that it's unimportant, discard it and move on. But at least check it out.

CHAPTER 6

MEDITATE TO PREPARE TO FIGHT

"Give me six hours to chop down a tree and I will
spend the first four sharpening the axe."
—Abraham Lincoln

Controlling The Negative Effects

Military training has always focused on the mind to
learn the intricacies of combat: weapons, First Aid,
communication, squad, platoon, and company tactics, and
how to follow orders and carry on though physically and
mentally drained. But the military is only now beginning
to understand the power of meditation to shape the brain
muscle to limit the negative effects of what a soldier
experiences on the battlefield.

Law enforcement agencies are slower to recognize
the power of preparing the mind for battle. While
many are doing an excellent job of helping officers heal
psychologically *after* a traumatic incident, they aren't doing
as good a job at teaching them to control their minds in the
heat of battle.

Some martial art schools prepare students for training with a few moments of quiet meditation and then conclude with another brief session. This is good. But most martial artists are poorly trained, if trained at all, to understand what happens to them mentally and physically when their training is suddenly and explosively put on the line.

I'm not going to preach to the choir here and tell you that under combat conditions your mental facilities can go berserk, whether facing withering gun fire from an Afghanistan village, a "kill the cops" screaming mob of rioters on a city street, or facing an opponent in the ring or on a street corner who you're convinced is violently insane.

Meditation helps

Meditation will help you to remain calm and focused in violent and chaotic situations. With regular sessions, cops and soldiers are less likely to fire out of fear, frustration, or hypervigilance. Also, warriors engaged in hand-to-hand combat are less likely to use force beyond what is necessary to end a situation. By practicing simple meditation techniques, you're less likely to overreact, freak out, or freeze, and far more likely to remain in the present moment to assess and then do what needs to be done appropriately.

Meditation helps you to see those incoming rounds, an enraged throng of rioters, or that toothless, tattooed sociopath, and not be overwhelmed by it. Instead, you're better able to think:

- I'm being shot at. From where? How can I stop this threat?
- We're about to be attacked by a mob or rioters. How can we control it? Stop it?
- I'm about to fight this behemoth. Where are his weaknesses? What is the best way to defeat him?

Instead of being overwhelmed by the enormity of the threat, you can better see the elements, and focus on the problem and the solution.

For the scientifically inclined reader, here is why: Studies show that meditation increases your gray-matter volume and bolsters synapses (gaps between nerve ends) in the brain's pre-frontal cortex, which improves attention and helps put an event in context, rather than letting the amygdala (your brain's fight-or-flight center) takeover your body's reaction to combat situations.

My friend Sonny, a veteran martial artist, said this about his meditation:

"Prior to each karate session, Master Hisataka would have us sit on our haunches and breathe slowly and deeply, endeavoring to enter a relaxed meditative state. Each training session would end similarly. Throughout the decades of training since, I would be presented with many methods of meditation, but to this day I return to this basic technique of deep breathing, emptying my mind of all thought. This has provided me with enormous instincts to calmly respond to stressful situations, not to overreact to them. This technique has kept me alive in various hot environments, as well as through numerous physical rehab programs and a bout with prostate cancer."

Resiliency

Dictionary.com defines resiliency as "the power or ability to return to the original form, position, etc., *after being bent, compressed, or stretched.*

For sure, combat can make you feel bent, compressed, or stretched, and a whole lot of other adjectives too.

On one occasion, three other officers and I responded to a shooting in which a man shot his doctor multiple times in the head with a shotgun, then reloaded to shoot more into his chest. At one point, we confronted the still armed, blood-splattered shooter, and quickly overpowered him and took him to the floor. As I cuffed the suspect, one of the officers freaked, mumbling repeatedly how he nearly shot the man. Seeing that the officer was about to hyperventilate, I slapped his shoulder and told him to help me cuff the suspect. That's all it took. The officer immediately snapped back to the moment and finished the job.

But what would have happened if we hadn't overpowered the shooter and he had fired at us? The officer's lack of resiliency, that is, his inability "to return to the original form after being bent and compressed," could have been disastrous.

Let's begin by looking at a few simple meditations to increase your awareness in a combat situation. Then we will look at meditation techniques and affirmations to help strengthen your resiliency in an unpredictable and potentially toxic combat situation.

Increasing Your Awareness

One veteran soldier of the war in Iraq said that too many times he would find his mind wandering while he was on patrol in some hot, dusty city. He said that instead of watching people, he would wonder what he would have for chow later. It was when he began having these wayward thoughts every time he went out on a mission that he looked into meditation to develop better focus. He said that it didn't take many sessions before he was better able to stay on task.

Veteran martial artist and writer, Christopher Caile, says this about the value of meditation in preparation for battle:

> *"Over time, just sitting can produce internal changes that transform normal perceptions and awareness and develop them beyond the norm. Your concentration evolves toward a state of total focused awareness that allows the slightest nuance of perception or intuition to be acknowledged and not be clouded by prior experience, or filtered out by distraction or inattentiveness, or colored by emotion."*

Let's begin with a meditation that will increase your awareness of everything around you, as well as what is going on inside of you.

General Awareness Meditation

Standing meditation

Before we get to the actual meditation, let's look at how to do standing meditation. The good news is that it's simple and doesn't draw any attention to yourself should you want to do it around people.

How to do it:

- **Classic:** The classic way is to stand with your feet about shoulder-width apart, back and head straight, with your hands held comfortably just below your navel. The back of your right hand rests gently in the palm of your left, the tips of your thumbs touch.
- Your eyes are closed or open; it's your choice.
- **Casual:** The casual way is to stand with your hands in your pockets or hanging at your sides.
- You can stand out in the open, next to your squad car, or beside a BOB striking dummy. In short, you can do it anywhere as long as you have a few minutes to yourself.
- The only real requirement is that you stand in good balance, and your posture and head are straight, or straightish. You want to focus on your meditation, so you don't want to be off balance or falling over.

Meditating on internal feelings

This is a standing meditation in which you will perceive different stimuli and increase your awareness of certain sensations, feelings, and emotions about them. Hey, get back here. This isn't as touch-feely as it might sound.

By becoming more mindful of sensations, feelings, and emotions, you become increasingly aware of everything around you. If possible, do this barefoot.

Here is how to do it.

Become aware of sensations:

- Stand in place for a moment and focus your eyes on the ground about 10 feet in front of you.
- Take a few moments to focus on your slow, deep inhalation and slow exhalation. Each time you exhale think *calm, relax,* or *sink.*
- Become aware of all the muscles in your body involved in keeping you upright. *Feel* how this muscle subtly adjusts you one way and *feel* how that muscle adjusts you another.
- *Feel* your feet on the ground or floor. *Feel* the texture of the surface on your feet. Is it rough, smooth, cold, or warm?
- If you're outside, do you *feel* the sun or wind against your body? If you're inside, do you *feel* cold, warm, or hot?
- With your eyes still *fixed* on the ground 10 feet in front of you, what do you *see*?
- What do you *smell*?
- What do you *hear*?

As always, don't pass judgment on any of the sensory perceptions. Just be aware of them.

Become aware of your feelings:

- As you stand motionless, do you feel comfortable or uncomfortable?
- Do you feel relaxed or are you full of tension?
- How do you feel about what you see, hear and smell?
- How do you feel about this meditation experience?

When answering how you feel about something, simply answer and move on. Don't loiter on a feeling and don't pass judgment on it more than giving yourself a simple answer. *I hear a passing airplane; it sounds like a big one. I smell exhaust; it must be a truck.* Don't try to fix something. For example, if you feel uncomfortable, just observe the feeling—*My right foot hurts today*—and move on to another feeling.

Become aware of your emotions:

- Do you feel happy or sad?
- Do you feel calm or fearful?
- Are you feeling angry of peaceful?
- What other emotions do you feel?

Again, don't pass judgment on what you feel and don't try to fix anything. Simply observe.

Now observe if there are connections between your sensations, feelings, and emotions. Does one affect the other? *That truck exhaust is thick and it's burning my eyes.* Just be aware of the connections without fixing them. Just observe and leave it alone.

Walking Meditation

Walking meditation is a nice break from sitting for long periods. It's also a way to meditate around others without them knowing about it, such as when manning a post, waiting on the sidelines to compete, or waiting backstage to give a speech. The only hitch to looking natural is that walking meditation is done slowly.

Choose any meditation method described in the book that will work when walking. Here are two walking methods. First the classic followed by the causal.

Here is how to do it:

The classic:

- Stand with your feet side-by-side, your hands positioned at about your navel, the back of your left hand resting gently in the palm of your right, and the tips of your thumbs touching.
- Step forward with your right foot, landing first on your heel, and slowly lower it to the ground.
- Breathe in as your heel touches. Because you take a deep breath into your lower belly, your heel may be poised on its back edge for 4 or 5 seconds.
- Breathe out as the rest of your foot lowers to the floor, which will take about 5 or 6 seconds.
- Move your left foot forward, inhaling slowly as your heel sets down on the back edge.
- Exhale as the rest of your foot settles slowly onto the floor.

For the first 5 minutes or so, focus only on your breathing. Inhale as you lower your heel to the ground and exhale as the rest of your foot touches down.

Once you feel comfortable that you have a nice rhythm to your stepping and breathing, you want to become aware of:

- your body movements.
- the sensation of the ground on your feet.
- the distribution of your weight as you step so very slowly.
- your back posture.
- the sensation of the clothes on your body.
- the temperature of where you are (cold wind in your face, warm sun on your back).

The casual:

The casual walking method is the same—breathe in as your heel touches the earth or floor and exhale as you slowly lower the rest of your foot to the surface.

If you want to put your hands in your pockets or slowly move them as you normally do when walking, that's fine. Keep your back and neck straight, your eyes open or closed.

Follow the steps as listed for the classic.

Whether you use the classic walking method or the casual, don't try to fix anything that happens. If you step on a sharp stone or you bang your shin on a coffee table, so be it. Don't label your walk as good or bad; it is what it is. If a car honks or your phone rings, observe the sensations, feelings, and emotions you experience from the sound, and move on.

Walking meditation forces you to become aware of yourself and aware of your surroundings, both critically important in high-stress, combat situations.

Here is another.

Five Sounds, Five Touches

Author and personal safety expert Rory Miller taught this method to me. It's an excellent way to center yourself and a way to increase your awareness of your surroundings. It's all about being completely focused in the moment.

Here is how it's done:

- Sit, stand, lie or walk.
- Close your eyes all the way, close them partially, or open them.
- To prepare your mind, inhale slowly and deeply, and exhale slowly. Repeat two or three more times.
- Take a few minutes to follow your breath to bring on a sense of calm and quiet.
- Begin by focusing on sounds, five of them. For example, this is what I hear right now. Inside my office, I hear soft, classical music playing on my sound system. Outdoors I can hear a neighbor's dog barking, a garbage truck on the next street over, an airplane descending toward the airport and, I need one more…there it is. A squirrel chattering in a tree.
- Now, focus on your sense of touch, five of them. Here are mine. I can feel my butt getting tired of sitting, my forearms touching the front edge of my desk, my fingertips tapping out these words, my glasses resting on my nose, and the weight of my sweatshirt on my shoulders.

Don't pass judgment on any of these things. Don't think: *That barking dog is so annoying. My butt will never be the same.* Simply acknowledge them, and move on to the next one.

While this is a meditation technique to help you increase your awareness, it's not too much of a stretch to see how this could help you in a combat situation, especially in darkness.

Key points:

- Keep your eyes closed throughout the meditation.
- Stay in the moment as you acknowledge each sound and touch.
- Don't judge the sound and touch, just hear it, feel it, and move on to the next.
- Do more than five of each if you wish. Or acknowledge five sounds and five touches, and then acknowledge five new sounds and five new touches.

Hole In A Cardboard Meditation

I learned this in a Zen monastery as a way to increase concentration. Little did they know they were also teaching this old warrior a way to expand his awareness.

We used a piece of cardboard, but you can easily use a piece of typing paper. Cut a hole in the center of it about the size of a quarter. Sit on the floor and place the cardboard flat in front of you so that the hole is about 18 inches away from your folded legs.

Here is how you do it:

- Sit on the floor or on a chair.
- Close your eyes all the way, close them partially, or open them.
- Use your trigger word or 4-count tactical breathing to begin the calming process.
- Take a few minutes to follow your breath and bring on a sense of calm and quiet.
- Open your eyes and look at the hole in the cardboard. Without passing judgment, let your eyes travel around the inside of it, noting its size and shape.
- Now look into the hole and observe what is inside: carpet, grass, wood. Don't let your eyes move away from the hole.
- After a moment, without moving your eyes from the hole, expand your perception outward two or three inches. Use your peripheral vision to see whatever you can see. It might be a flaw in the cardboard, a spot of some kind on the floor, or just more cardboard. Don't judge it. Simply expand your perception.

- After a couple of minutes, expand your perception to the four sides of the cardboard. Do this without moving your eyes from the hole. Observe the edges without judgment.
- After a couple of minutes, expand your perception six inches beyond the four sides. Don't look directly at them. Keep your eyes trained on the hole and use your peripheral vision. They're probably blurry but concentrate on what you can perceive.
- After a couple of minutes, without moving your eyes from the hole, expand your perception as far as it goes. Don't judge what you "see." Just be aware.
- The last step is to try to see farther than your peripheral. If you're doing this in a familiar setting, know the difference between remembering that there is a tree to your right or a table to your left, and really perceiving a blurred perception of it.
- Take your time.

Key points:

- In the description I say "after a couple of minutes" before moving on to the next step. Feel free to stay where you are longer than two minutes. Sometime I'll stay 5 minutes or even longer. Focus and strive to see as widely and with as much clarity as you can.
- Clearly, the better your peripheral vision, and your awareness of all that is within it, is a valuable skill in a combat scenario.

Nail On The Wall

Here is a slight variation on the "Hole in cardboard meditation." Let's say that you hate cardboard or you don't want to sit on the floor or ground. No problem. You can easily do the same meditation while focusing on a nail in the wall, a knot in a tree, or a small mark on the side of a vehicle.

Sit in a chair or vehicle, or stand, and follow the steps as described in "Hole in cardboard meditation." Take your time, expand your perception progressively, and stay focused on the task.

Key points:

There is no rush in the various steps. If you want to remain longer than two minutes on any of them, that's fine.

- Each time you do the meditation, strive to perceive more and more out of your peripheral vision.
- Can you do the exercise without using meditation to calm and clear your mind? Yes. However, the advantage in meditating first is that it quiets your mind so that you can better focus all of your attention on being aware of your visual perception.

Samurai Meditation

Here is one more variation of "Hole in cardboard meditation." Purportedly, the samurai used it just before going into battle because it gave them immediate results.

Here is how you do it:

- Sit anywhere you like and get comfortable. If you're new to this meditation, it's best to choose a place that is quiet and with few distractions.
- Close your eyes all the way, close them partially, or open them.
- To prepare your mind, inhale slowly and deeply, and exhale slowly. Repeat two or three more times. Take a few minutes to follow your breath and bring on a sense of calm and quiet.

Now that you're ready, you're going to focus on an object.

- Find something small in your line of sight and focus on it. Observe its size, color, texture and shape. Don't pass judgment; simply observe.
- After a couple of minutes and without moving your eyes from the object, soften your gaze and strive to perceive as far as you can below it, above it, to the right of it, and to the left. Don't move your eyes from the object.
- Now, snap your head to the right or left, and stop and fix your eyes on another object, focusing on it just as you did on the first one. Notice that your peripheral vision is better now and that you can perceive more quickly in all four directions than you did the first time.
- Snap your head in the other direction, and stop your eyes on an object. Again perceive quickly all that you can without moving your eyes.

Key points:

* Strive to perceive more and more each time you do the meditation.
* Can you do the exercise without using meditation to calm and clear your mind? Yes. But using a meditation method of your choice quiets your mind so that you can better focus all of your attention on being aware of your visual perception.
* This method enhances your ability to perceive widely, which ultimately carries over into a combat situation.

Affirmations For Combat

As mentioned above, too many people repeat in their minds negative words and declarations about situations and their ability to function in them. Subsequently, they create undesirable outcomes. As discussed, words and declarations work both ways: one destroys and the other builds positively. In short, it's how you use words that determine the results.

When preparing for combat, never is your choice of words—whether spoken aloud to others or thought to yourself—more important. Remember, your subconscious mind accepts as true what you say or think. It listens to what you tell it—whether negative or positive—and guides you on that specific path.

Fortunately, the solution is simple: Keep all negativity out of what you say and think. Choose only positive statements so that you get positive results. Meditation, and the relaxed state it brings to your mind, is the perfect vehicle to ingrain positivity into your head, and ultimately into your actions.

Here is how to start the ingraining:

- Sit anywhere you like and get comfortable. If you're new to this meditation, it's best to choose a place that is quiet with few distractions.
- Close your eyes all the way, close them partially, or open them.
- To prepare your mind, inhale slowly and deeply, and exhale slowly. Repeat two or three more times.

Choose a meditation method to get deeply relaxed. Then proceed through the following.

Say aloud, whisper, or think the following affirmations. Hear the words in your mind and pause at the end to think what they mean to you. It doesn't matter what anyone else thinks they mean; it's all about you right now.

Below find affirmations for martial artists, law enforcement, and soldiers. If you're, say, a soldier and see one under "martial arts" or "law enforcement" that works for you, steal it and make it your own.

Affirmations for martial arts:

- I'm a confident martial artist.
- I'm a powerful fighter.
- I'm fast.
- My reflexes are instantaneous.
- My mind is clear.
- I'll only fight the opponent (meaning you won't be intimidated by his belt, tattoos, muscles, or veiny forehead).
- My punches are explosive.
- My kicks are accurate.
- I'm calm.
- I'm anxious to compete.
- I handle pressure easily.
- I'm excited to win.

Affirmations for law enforcement:

- I'm a good police officer.
- I'm an excellent communicator.
- I'm confident in my skills.
- I have excellent officer survival skills.
- I respond with force when necessary.
- I'm skilled at defensive tactics.
- I'm skilled with firearms.
- I'm calm in chaotic situations.
- I'm skilled at helping my fellow officers to remain calm.
- I'll fight all-out when it's needed.
- I'll continue to fight though I'm injured.
- I'll continue to fight as long as I can draw a breath.

Affirmations for soldiers

- I'm confident in my training.
- I'm confident in my skillset.
- I'm skilled with numerous weapons.
- There will be noise and confusion and I will be in control.
- I know what I am supposed to do.
- I can function though I am frightened.
- Fear sharpens my mind and steadies my hand.
- I'll be in control under fire.
- I'll follow orders.
- I'll fight for my buddy on my left and my buddy on my right.
- I'll continue to fight though I'm injured.
- I'll continue to fight as long as I can draw a breath.

Key points:

- Don't think or say the words without deeply understanding their meaning. These positively structured sentences will guide your action but only if you contemplate their meaning.
- If one or more of the above sentences don't reflect how you would say or think them, simply change them to fit your voice. Just remember to keep them positive. For example, don't say, "I won't lose control under fire." State it positively: "I will be in control under fire."
- If the above examples don't completely satisfy your needs, simply add sentences that do.

Mental Imagery For A Successful Conclusion

Here is a simple meditation method to place into your mind a clear picture of a successful conclusion of your mission, tour, or fight.

For soldiers

I was sitting in my parent's house the day before I was to leave for Oakland, California to fly to Vietnam. My muscles were twitching, my eyes were watering, and I couldn't sit still. My mother was in the kitchen and I was sitting in the living room on the couch, nervously twisting a doily, and wondering if I'd ever see the room again.

As brilliant as a camera flash, I suddenly got a clear mental picture of me sitting in the same spot, 12 months later, and playing with that doily. Call it an epiphany, a Psychic Network moment, or just wishful thinking, but at that moment I knew—*I knew*—that it would happen. To use the vernacular of those times, there was no question in my military mind that I would be sitting right there a year later.

Twelve months later, and there I was on one end of the sofa, twisting my mother's doily and getting chewed out for it. I don't remember now if I thought about that mental image during my time in Vietnam, but a year later, it popped back in mind the moment I sat down.

In the Vietnam War there was a phenomena that a lot of soldiers experienced that went by many names. I knew it as the "The Vietnam Blues." It was that point in one's tour in which the reality of home became unclear. Foggy. Fuzzy.

Cloaking it in high definition clarity was the war, and all its incredible intensity.

While I didn't place my image of home into my mind via meditation that day at my parent's, I like to think my sudden epiphany burned it into my subconscious to some degree. Might it have guided me those 12 months?

One veteran of Afghanistan told me that he would image a shorter time objective, and that works too. He said:

"I would first use the 4-count breathing technique to calm myself [see Chapter 4]. *I would then picture in my mind how I would feel after whatever stressful situation I was about to encounter was over. I would make myself remember that the situation—whether having to wake up at 4 a.m. in the freezing cold for kitchen duty after having finally fallen asleep at 3 a.m., or preparing to go on a patrol into an area known to be Taliban hunting grounds—would eventually have an ending. No matter how intense, or how dangerous, or how exhausting, it couldn't last forever. Imagining this, trying to put myself in the place of the event already being over, would almost always make me feel more relaxed."*

How to do it:

- Sit, stand, lie or walk.
- Close your eyes all the way, close them partially, or open them.
- To prepare your mind, inhale slowly and deeply, and exhale slowly. Repeat two or three more times.

Choose a meditation method to get deeply relaxed.

- Meditate to bring on a sense of calm and quiet. The more deeply you go, the more receptive your mind to suggestions and imagery.
- Create a vivid image in your mind of your homecoming.
    - your plane landing on a military base.
    - you being greeted at the airport by family and friends.
    - you being greeted by your dog.
    - you walking into your parent's or your spouse's home.
- Tell yourself that you will see this ultra-clear image often on your deployment and that it will guide you.
- Tell yourself that you *will* experience this image upon your safe return.

Law enforcement

Law enforcement officers can also implant mental imagery of getting off shift. Each time you meditate, take a moment to see yourself at the end of your shift doing whatever you do: going home, going for a workout, or stopping for a brew. Whatever it is, see it clearly in your mind's eye.

You can do this even when you're meditating on another objective. Let's say that for the past two weeks you have been meditating on imaging the act of handcuffing smoothly.

Image the intricacies of the procedure as many times as you normally do. Then to conclude your meditation, image yourself finishing your shift.

Here is how to do it:

- Sit, stand, lie or walk.
- Close your eyes all the way, close them partially, or open them.
- To prepare your mind, inhale slowly and deeply, and exhale slowly. Repeat two or three more times.

Choose a meditation method to get deeply relaxed.

- Meditate to bring on a sense of calm and quiet. The more deeply you go, the more receptive your mind to suggestions and imagery.
- Create a vivid image in your mind of the end of your shift or the conclusion of a dangerous mission.
  - you filling out paperwork.
  - you changing back into your civvies.
  - you driving home.
  - you driving to the gym.
  - you greeting your spouse and kids.

For martial artists:

Martial artist can use mental imagery to implant the end of a competition or the end of grueling all-day seminar. Each time you meditate, take a moment to see yourself doing whatever you do after competition or after a hard workout. Maybe you look forward to a hot muscle-relaxing shower or a fun meal with your workout buddies. Whatever it is, see it clearly in your mind's eye.

How to do it:

- Sit, stand, lie or walk.
- Close your eyes all the way, close them partially, or open them.
- To prepare your mind, inhale slowly and deeply, and exhale slowly. Repeat two or three more times.

Choose a meditation method to get deeply relaxed.

- Meditate to bring on a sense of calm and quiet. The more deeply you go, the more receptive your mind to suggestions and imagery.
- Create a vivid image in your mind of the end of your event.
  - o   you hitting the shower.
  - o   you talking with your friends after the fight.
  - o   you talking to your fellow classmates after the tough workout.
  - o   you flopping on the sofa at home with your TV remote.
- Tell yourself that you *will* experience this image upon the completion of your fight or training.
- Tell yourself that no matter the outcome of the competition and no matter how you did at the seminar, you benefited from the experience. You learned and you grew as a martial artist.

Note: Some soldiers and law enforcement officers argue that they don't want anything to remind them of home and family while engaged in their duties. They believe it's distracting, and they want their mission to be the only thing on their minds. If that is how they believe, no one should try to change them. Likewise, they should not try to change someone's mind who does want to ingrain an image of coming home or getting off work.

In short, warriors must do what is right for them.

CHAPTER 7

MEDITATE AFTER THE FIGHT

"I have had to fight like hell and fighting like hell has made me what I am." ~ John Arbuthnot Fisher

After the battle can be a time of relief, giddiness, exhilaration, or mental suffering. Sometimes it might be all these and a few more. Also, you might still be experiencing an adrenaline rush, or it might have left your body so fast after the fight that now you feel like wilted lettuce.

How you feel might not be the same as how your buddy feels, or it might be identical. Whatever feelings and emotions you're experiencing is a normal reaction to an abnormal event.

It's been my experience that everyone deals with these things differently. One person might be traumatized by a brief, self-defense situation, but a soldier who just experienced a 30-minute firefight might feel fine. I saw one cop after he had wrestled a drunk into his backseat more shook than the one I saw the day before who had shot a knife-wielding drug dealer. Today you're fine after a fight but tomorrow you're not. It's just the way it is.

Whatever you feel is normal. It's the situation that was abnormal.

Meditation is helpful, whether you just dealt with a resist arrest situation, a sparring match where tempers flared, a bar fight, or a street battle in the war. In extreme cases of psychological trauma after an event, it's important to talk with someone, especially if you're having problems (See Chapter 8: "Post traumatic incident meditation").

After your incident, use any meditation in this book (or from any other source) that relaxes and calms you. Do it as soon as you can and as often as you can. In particular, refer to the meditations in Chapter 4: "Meditate to achieve a powerful sense of calm."

4-count breathing

In addition to your calming meditations, do three cycles of 4-count breathing (Chapter 4: "Meditate to achieve a powerful sense of calm") several times a day. It takes only about three minutes, but it goes a long way toward calming your anxiety and lowering your blood pressure.

If you use 4-count breathing as one of your longer meditation methods, do the three cycle version during other times.

Trigger word

Think or whisper your trigger word (Chapter Three: "Nuts and Bolts") to yourself several times a day to experience a pleasant sense of calming. Do this in addition to your meditation sessions.

SECTION II: CHAPTER 7   137

Affirmations

Repeating powerful affirmations to yourself (Chapter 6: "Meditate to prepare to fight") while in a meditative state will help to reduce anxiety and get you back on the right track. Remember to keep all negativity out of what you say and think. Use positive statements to get positive results.

Here is how to do it:

- Choose a place to sit or stand that is quiet with few distractions, and get comfortable.
- Close your eyes all the way, close them partially, or keep them open.
- To prepare your mind, inhale slowly and deeply, and exhale slowly. Repeat two or three more times.

Choose a meditation method to get deeply relaxed. Then proceed.

Say aloud, whisper, or think the following affirmations. Hear the words in your mind and pause at the end to think what they mean to you. It doesn't matter what anyone else thinks they mean; it's all about you right now.

- I survived the fight.
- I'm okay.
- What I'm feeling is normal.
- What I'm feeling is temporary.
- It will pass.
- I'm recovering.
- I'm feeling calmer now.
- So very calm.
- I'm in control of myself.
- I'm strong.
- I'm a warrior.

If these don't quite fit your situation, change them so that they do. Just remember to keep the statements positive.

Key Points:

• Continue to meditate, do 4-count breathing throughout the day, and/or think or whisper your trigger word throughout the day, and repeat your affirmations until you feel that you're where you want to be in your head.

• Should you have long lasting issues—nightmares, flashbacks, anxiety, hypervigilance, eating problems, and others—seek professional help as soon as you're able.

CHAPTER 8

POST TRAUMATIC INCIDENT MEDITATION

"Find a place inside where there's joy, and the joy
will burn out the pain" ~ Joseph Campbell

The *Diagnostic and Statistical Manual – IV*, published by
the American Psychiatric Association, is used all over
the country to define psychological injuries and mental
disorders. In it, a traumatic event is described as "the person
experienced, witnessed, or was confronted with an event or
events that involved actual or threatened death or serious
injury, or a threat to the physical integrity of self or others.
The person's response involved intense fear, helplessness,
or horror."

Post traumatic stress disorder (PTSD) can be defined as
a normal reaction to an abnormal event. While breaking
a bone isn't consider normal, no one would be surprised
if you received at least one after getting struck by a car.
Similarly, PTSD is a bruised psyche that has experienced
the psychological equivalent of being hit by one.

Exposure to a traumatic event—and this is key—will not always result in PTSD, just as getting hit by a car doesn't always result in major physical injury. In *Deadly Force Encounters,* published by Paladin Press, coauthor Dr. Alexis Artwohl and I list the many symptoms of PTSD. I'm not going to list them here because that would be beyond the scope of a book on meditation. But here are the four categories:

1. Exposure to a traumatic event.
2. Intrusive, persistent reliving of the trauma.
3. Avoidance of reminders of the event and numbing of general responsiveness.
4. Persistent symptoms of increased arousal.

Know that you don't have PTSD unless you're still experiencing the many symptoms that fall within each of these categories for more than a month after the event. If you experience anything the first month, it will be "acute stress disorder," meaning you're having a temporary reaction to a highly stressful and traumatic event. There is a reasonable chance that you will return to normal within a month.

Consider these statistics:

• One-third of police officers involved in a deadly force encounter will experience a mild reaction and will quickly return to normal.
• One-third will go on to develop a moderate reaction.
• One-third will develop severe reaction.

Even if a person doesn't develop the exact symptoms of PTSD, the event can put them at risk for a host of other problems, such as alcohol and drug abuse, social isolation, poor job performance, sexual problems, chronic physical illnesses, and many more.

It's important, therefore, that you talk with a mental health expert after an event. Meditation can go a long ways toward helping you find a powerful sense of calm. But to reiterate, it's paramount that you seek professional help to deal with the specifics of the disorder.

I'm not a trained professional and therefore I won't offer anything here that can be construed as help for PTSD. If you believe that you might be experiencing it, I highly recommend that you seek professional help as soon as you can.

If for whatever reason you can't get help right away, you will find some comfort practicing any of the calming meditation techniques suggest throughout this book. However, even if you find calm and relaxation with meditation, you should still talk with a professional therapist.

CHAPTER 9

MEDITATE TO INDUCE SLEFP

Sleep is a symptom of caffeine deprivation ~ Anon

To be mentally sharp and alert, and to function at your best in training and in a combat situation, you need sleep to rest and recuperate your brain and muscles. The bad news for law enforcement officers, soldiers, and martial artists who work busy and stressful jobs, quality sleep is too often a scarcity. Sometimes the lack of it is a result of long work days, while other times you're just too keyed up to drift off.

While you might not have control over how much you get, here are some meditation techniques to help you drift off when you do have the opportunity.

Progressive Relaxation

Many people have found this simple meditation to be wonderfully helpful, including military test subjects. Many have found, as I have, that they fall asleep before finishing the meditation. And that's just fine. Don't hit a gift horse in the mouth.

Here is how you do it:

- Sit or lie down.
- Sit comfortably with your hands in your lap or on your thighs. If you're lying on your back, rest your hands along your sides or on your belly.
- Close your eyes all the way or close them partially.
- To prepare your mind, inhale slowly and deeply, and exhale slowly. Repeat two or three more times.
- Take a few minutes to follow your breath and bring on a sense of calm and quiet.

Now you're ready to progressively relax your body.

- Begin with your toes and feet. It doesn't matter if you're barefoot or wearing boots. Your objective is to focus on the sensations in your feet as you breathe in and out normally.
    - o Tense your toes and feet for about 10 seconds.
    - o Stop the tension, and for the next 20 seconds savor the sensation of relaxation that envelops your feet.
- Move your attention to your calves and shins.
    - o Tense them (without tensing your feet) for 10 seconds.
    - o Stop the tension, and for the next 20 seconds savor the sensation of relaxation that sweeps through your calves and shins.

- Move your attention to your upper legs, front and back.
  - ○ Tense them (without tensing your feet or lower legs) for 10 seconds.
  - ○ Stop the tension, and for the next 20 seconds savor the sensation of relaxation that sweeps through your legs.
- Move your attention to your hips, rear, and groin area.
  - ○ Tense them (without tensing your legs or feet) for 10 seconds.
  - ○ Stop the tension, and for the next 20 seconds savor the sensation of relaxation that sweeps through your hip area.
- Move your attention to your stomach muscles, sides and lower back.
  - ○ Tense them (without tensing your chest or hips) for 10 seconds.
  - ○ Stop the tension, and for the next 20 seconds savor the sensation of relaxation that sweeps through your lower torso.
- Move your attention to your chest and back.
  - ○ Tense them (without tensing your stomach, lower back or neck) for 10 seconds.
  - ○ Stop the tension, and for the next 20 seconds savor the sensation of relaxation that sweeps through your chest and back.
- Move your attention to your hands, forearms and upper arms.
  - ○ Tense them (without tensing your shoulders or neck) for 10 seconds.
  - ○ Stop the tension, and for the next 20 seconds savor the sensation of relaxation that sweeps through your arms.
- Move your attention to your shoulders, especially the muscles on top, the traps.
  - ○ Tense them (without tensing your face or neck) for 10 seconds.

      o   Stop the tension, and for the next 20 seconds savor the sensation of relaxation that sweeps through your shoulders.
- Move your attention to your neck and face.
      o   Tense them (without tensing your shoulders) for 10 seconds.
      o   Stop the tension, and for the next 20 seconds savor the sensation of relaxation that sweeps through your neck and face.

If you're still awake, take a few minutes to savor how incredibly relaxed your body feels. If one body part is still tense, put your mind there, contract its muscles for 10 seconds, and relax it again.

There are more advanced variations of this technique but this is a popular one in the military to bring on blessed sleep.

Key points:

- You don't have to tense your muscles so hard that they are quivering and you're sweating profusely. Mild tension will suffice.
- Practice these techniques even when you're enjoying a spell of good quality sleep so that you're versed in them when insomnia, fatigue, and irritability are once again disturbing your rest.
- If it helps you relax more, take a minute or two between each body part to focus on following your breath in and out.
- At the beginning of each body part, whisper or think your trigger word two or three times.

Abdominal Breathing

Don't you love it when you're having a hard time sleeping multiple nights in a row and some bozo advises you to "just relax?" Instead of driving your Hummer over the guy's face, try this easy-to-do meditation that includes a breathing technique you can do throughout the day.

Practice this just before you get into bed or after you've gotten into it. As a general stress reliever, you can also do it at your desk, in your squad, or in the back of a truck. One soldier said that because privacy was at a premium when he was deployed, he would practice this technique for a few minutes when visiting the porta-potty.

This is similar to some of those above but with an additional focus on your hands.

Here is how you do it:

- While sitting or lying down in bed, close your eyes and place your hands on your belly to feel the gentle rising and falling. This isn't a time to think about your mission or ways to improve your sidekick. Now it's all about your breathing.
- In your mind, feel your hands on your stomach: the backs of them, your palms, your thumbs, and your fingers.
- Inhale slowly and deeply into your belly. Feel your stomach rise and your hands go along for the ride. Think only of this.
- Exhale slowly. Feel your stomach sink and feel your hands descend with it. Think only of this.

Repeat this as many times as you like. If you fall asleep in the middle of it, don't worry. You will keep breathing.

Key points:

• The exhale phase is believed to be more relaxing than the inhale—because you're letting go and sinking with the release of the breath—so it's important to stay mindful during this phase.

• Focus on inhaling and exhaling slowly, but not so slowly that it's uncomfortable.

• Because you always have with you your body and your breathing, you can do this simple method anywhere and anytime you have a moment throughout the day. Simply get comfortable with your hands on your stomach, close your eyes, and feel your belly and hands rise and fall with your breathing. Do it for at least a minute.

• If closing your eyes might bring unwanted attention from your boss, your sergeant, or your coworker (or passengers in your car), keep them open while focusing on your breathing. It's harder that way, but if it's the only way you can do it, it's better than letting stress dictate how you feel.

• Practice this simple meditation two or three times during the day, or however many times you can do it. Then do it once again just at bedtime.

"Sink"

I call this method "sink" because the word works for me. Please try it, but if you discover another word that works better for you—"fall," "drop," "melt," soften"—by all means change it. Either think your word or whisper it on each exhalation. Do this meditation sitting or lying down because your objective is to sink into your bed and pillow, or into a comfortable chair.

Here is how to do it:

- Sit or lie.
- Close your eyes all the way or close them partially.
- To prepare your mind, inhale slowly and deeply, and exhale slowly. Repeat two or three more times.
- Take a few minutes to follow your breath to bring on a sense of calm and quiet.
- When you're ready, inhale slowly and deeply, and exhale slowly as you think or whisper "sink," or another word you like.
- Each time you think or whisper your word, feel yourself sink more deeply into your mattress and pillow, or chair.
- On each exhalation, mentally feel your body and head grow heavier, more relaxed, and sink deeper and deeper.
- Repeat this simple procedure until you fall asleep.

Key points:

- It's important that you feel yourself sink more deeply each time you exhale. Use your imagination to feel and even see yourself descending into whatever you're lying on or sitting on.
- Don't rush the process. This is all about relaxing your mind and body to bring on some serious shuteye.

CHAPTER 10

THREE 1-MINUTE MEDITATIONS

"How long a minute is depends on what side of the bathroom door you're on." ~ Anon

Many people find that they enjoy one-minute meditations so much that they do them several times throughout their busy day. Great! We're only talking 60 seconds and who doesn't have a minute to spare two or three times a day?

I know a couple of people who work insanely busy jobs. So once or twice a day, they pin their desk phone between their necks and their ears and pretend to be listening to someone for a minute. With no one on the other end of the line, they use the 60 seconds to mentally calm and collect themselves.

Here are three examples of one-minute meditations. Many people do them to enjoy a sort of "vacation," in which they instill in themselves a sense of calm and relaxation

Here is how you do it:

Meditation 1: Focus on an object

For 60 seconds you're to meditate on an object. It can be your martial arts belt, your weapon, your shoulder patch, whatever. This meditation clears your mind of all other thoughts as you focus on one thing, for one brief moment.

- Sit, take a deep breath, and let it out slowly.
- Look at the object in front of you and focus only on it, allowing it to fill all of your awareness.
- Should you be distracted, gently return your focus on the object.
- Identify one quality of that object: a loose thread on your belt, a ridge or groove on the side of your weapon, or a single letter or symbol on your patch.
- Focus all of your attention on it.
- Hold that one thought.

Meditation 2: Just relax

For 60 seconds, relax your body and mind as deeply as you can.

- Stop and sit or stand completely still.
- Breathe in slowly and exhale slowly.
- On each inhalation, think, "I'm calm and I'm composed." Strive to feel that calmness and composure.
- On each exhalation, whisper or think, "My mind and body are relaxed." Feel a sense of relaxation wash over your body.

Meditation 3: See yourself succeeding

For 60 seconds, see yourself succeeding at one part of an activity: shooting five rounds into the bullseye; scoring the perfect sidekick; extracting a resisting driver from a vehicle.

- Sit or stand, and slowly take in a deep breath and slowly exhale it.
- See yourself calmly and with complete control, doing your activity.
- If you can do your activity more than once in 60 seconds, do so…

CONCLUSION

Are we born to the warrior life or did the warrior life choose us? It's a question that has been debated for a long time and will likely continue to be so.

The warrior life takes its toll on one's body and mind. I've seen it in others and I've experienced it myself. I've seen it destroy men and women who were exemplary warriors because for any number of reasons they were not helped.

Happily, the warrior community is finally recognizing that those who face the dragon with well-honed skills must be taught ways to mentally prepare for battle, survive it, and survive the haunting aftermath.

One powerful device that is rapidly being included in the warrior community tool box is the power of meditation. The greatest roadblock to its acceptance is the erroneous belief by those in the uninformed camp that meditation is supernatural, New Age, Eastern mumbo jumbo, or just plain b.s..

Happily, the ever growing informed camp is accepting meditation as the powerful warrior tool that it is.

I sincerely hope this small guide took some of the mysticism out of meditation and gave you ways to find a quiet place within.

"*The mind can be our best friend and advocate in getting what we want in life, or it can pull the brakes on and be a nasty little foe—the choice is yours—choose your attitude.*"

– Rachael Bermingham

ABOUT THE AUTHOR

Loren W. Christensen is a Vietnam veteran and retired police officer with 29 years of law enforcement experience. As a martial arts student and teacher since 1965, he has earned a total of 11 black belts in three arts and was inducted into the Masters Hall of Fame in 2011. He has starred in seven instructional martial arts DVDs.

As a writer, Loren has worked with five publishers, penning 45 nonfiction books on a variety of subjects, a thriller fiction series called *Dukkha*, and dozens of magazine articles.

He can be contacted through his website:

www.lwcbooks.com

Loren W. Christensen
DVDs

Solo Training
Fighting Dirty
Speed Training
Masters and Styles
Vital Targets
The Brutal Art of Ripping, and Pressing Vital Targets
Restraint and Control Strategies